OUT TO GET YOU

...of the people, by the people and ~~for~~
against the people

Dr. Ben A. Carlsen

"Here they come again
Insecure what you gonna do
Feel so small they could step on you"

From the song: *Out to Get You,* by *James*

OUT TO GET YOU

Dr. Ben A. Carlsen

New York, Miami, Los Angeles

OUT TO GET YOU
...of the people, by the people and ~~for~~ against the people

by Dr. Ben A. Carlsen

Copyright © 2013
ISBN no: 978-1-62847-601-9 (Hardcover)
       978-1-62847-602-6 (Paperback)
Library of Congress control no: 2013917071

Published by **Palm Springs Publishing**
New York, Miami, Los Angeles
Printed in U.S.A.

Website: outtogetyou.us

Cover Design by Gordon X. Drago

ACKNOWLEDGMENTS

--Special thanks to my family and friends who helped and/or stood by me in creating this book.

--Additional thanks to *Nick Smith* for writing the *Foreword*.

-- Thanks to *President Obama* and his predecessors for inadvertently providing me with so much material. And my appreciation to the great thinkers, philosophers, and leaders, deceased and alive, whose words I frequently quoted throughout the book.

--Apologies to President *Abraham Lincoln*, for liberties I took in changing one word of a portion of his *Gettysburg Address*, in the book's subtitle (although if he were alive today I believe he might concur).

...like many of you, I've become increasingly concerned about the direction and leadership of our country. Although I retain faith in our collective ability to change course and regain the preeminence— economically, socially, morally, and internationally that we once enjoyed-- and while some progress has been made on several fronts, the "American Dream" seems to be turning into a bad one...

--the author

CONTENTS

CHAPTERS

FOREWORD

Government of the people, for the people, and by the people is a phrase enshrined in our society from the early years of our great nation. The phrase packs so much into just 11 words. In 11 words, we break down the barriers between government and citizens. Government "for the people" presumably has the same motivations and goals as "the people" governed. Government "by the people" presumably uses the same strategies and tactics "the people" would use in governing. The problem with American government today is that while our elected leaders come from "the people," they are not "of the people."

A great divide exists between our elected leaders and the electorate. Rather than represent the public, elected leaders play a great trick on their constituents. Whether they serve in Congress, or even the White House, elected officials are not motivated by the public interest, or even special interests, rather they are motivated by self-interest.

The self-interest of our government is at the heart of Out to Get You. Dr. Ben Carlsen applies his extensive experience in business, finance, and education to expose the game played by American government in its current, perverted state. Carlsen's work is remarkable in today's atmosphere, because he does not write from a liberal or conservative viewpoint. He does not see the world in the vein of Republican and Democratic ideology. His analysis is hard-hitting, but it hits fairly, evenly, and without ulterior, political motives.

Before I ran for office myself, I had a conversation with Dr. Carlsen. He had a way of being both circumspect, and enthusiastic. When I lost my election, he gave me great insight into my campaign with his probative questions. One of the talents Dr. Carlsen possesses is the ability to speak to issues without bias. The average book buyer reads political books not for edification, but rather for confirmation of his or her own political viewpoints. Fire-throwers get attention and sell books.

It is rare to find a book about politics and government without the author's political bias evident from page one. <u>Out to Get You</u> is a refreshing departure from that tactic and therefore an important addition to the genre.

I recently spoke to my Congressman. He lamented that he could not get on television news programs, because he tended towards civility and moderation in his political discourse. It is a sad state of affairs when the only way to get attention is to make stupid and loud accusations and declarations. While <u>Out to Get You</u> is critical of American government and politics, Dr. Carlsen does not resort to cheap tricks of today's political pundits. His writing reflects his temperament and experience. He is not a politician. He is not a pundit. He is a businessman, an educator, and an author.

In all of my discussions with him I have always been impressed with his political independence. He writes like he talks. <u>Out to Get You</u> is not a book for Republicans or Democrats, Greens, or Libertarians. It is a book for Americans concerned with the direction of the country. I may not agree with everything Dr. Carlsen writes, but I always respect his information and insight.

The printing of the first edition of <u>Out to Get You</u> coincides with a period of intense and mindless political debate. The political atmosphere is as acrimonious as the ages of battles over desegregation and slavery. Dr. Carlsen addresses the prevalent issues of the day: healthcare, deficits, immigration, taxes, and entitlements. He lets you, the reader make your own decisions about each issue. He merely exposes the tricks the government plays on you in each issue of the day.

I hope you, the reader, take away as much from <u>Out to Get You</u> as I did. I hope you enjoy Dr. Carlsen's conversational style of writing. Most of all, I hope that you share the doctor's optimism in the face of what could easily be depressing news. The government is out to get you, after all.

Nicholas Smith, J.D.
Commonwealth of Virginia

INTRODUCTION

What if someone conspired to take away your income, disrupt your life, jeopardize your family, and make you live in a state of fear? What would you do? What if they also had almost unlimited power and weapons to scare and intimidate you? And what if they could make rules to limit your freedom? Would you be mad, frightened and rightfully concerned? Would you want to escape? Defend yourself? Neutralize them? Would you call the authorities?

What if they are the "authorities?"

Many Americans are concerned, uneasy, troubled and angry. Those of my generation often reflect and conclude: "This isn't the country I grew up in!"

What happened? How did we become so disillusioned and intimidated? And how did we become so poor?

This book expresses the concerns of many. Good solid citizens of every color and creed. People who believe in the American Dream. (Or perhaps I should use the past tense here.)

Who hijacked our Dream? Our future? Our security? Our sense of fairness? Our opportunities?

And what can we do about it?

I didn't plan on writing this book. The idea gradually washed over me, interestingly enough, and metaphorically accurate, while I was at my morning exercise routine on Miami Beach.

I always get my best ideas there, perhaps because as a friend of mine once said: "God lives at the Beach."

As I was contemplating writing this book I reflected on my background and qualifications. I'm an educator and consultant and I've had years of management experience in both the public and the private sector. I've also written several other books and enjoy research. I'm an avid follower of politics, economics and business, and I've voted in every election. However, perhaps my most important qualification for writing this book is: *I'm not, never have been, and never will be a Politician.* The nearest I ever got to that was CEO of a small college, President and Board Member of several professional associations, and President of my Condo Board.

My first step in preparing to write this book was trying to place my concerns about our government into some rational framework. We all kind of grumble about the government. Their inefficiency and ineffectiveness, their spendthrift ways and their apparent lack of concern about everyday issues confronting the American public. But my concerns ran much deeper. It's like they've been subverted, or have subordinated their primary purpose from *governing* to something else.

It seems to me our elected officials should be coming into the office every day, thinking: "How can I make things better for the American people?" Or, "What can I do to help the average person?" and "How can I make this a better country?" Kind of like a "Mr. Smith goes to Washington" mentality. Remember in this classic film how the patriotic, idealistic Mr. Smith (Joe Average) felt when he discovered how rare his values were in the halls of Congress? Making things better for the Country and its people seems so far down the list on our current politicians' agenda as to be practically undetectable.

I thought: These are down times in America: Socially, politically and economically. A sense of dispiritedness has gripped the land. I hear it in conversations with my friends, see evidence of it in the media, and observe it as I go about my daily activities.

I decided to write about it in the hopes that surfacing and discussing the main issues might just possibly shake people out of their lethargy and fear. And just might stir a few, and it will require many more, to advocate and press for change.

To the extent feasible I endeavored to use credible and accurate sources in compiling data and information. Journal articles, books, government websites, non-profit research organizations and newspapers such as the *New York Times*, *Washington Post*, *Los Angeles Times*, etc. As we know, statistics can be used to mis-inform as well as inform, so I voiced caution throughout the book. Part of my objective was to stimulate your interest and analysis, and enable you to put things into your personal framework and perspective. And, although like everyone, I have my personal biases, I have endeavored to be fair.

We generally see and hear clips on the evening news, on the internet, our radio station or in the newspapers. They seem like isolated incidents. A charge of corruption here, a case of malfeasance or bribery there. Sometimes bigger news like the *Benghazi* terrorist attack, or revelations by a former *CIA* employee. We often fail to connect the dots. In this book we'll attempt to connect some of the "dots," by examining some of the major issues and programs all in one place. There's a pattern. A pattern of corruption, ineptness, lying and manipulation. A culture of government gone wild. Apparently uncaring about the people or the country.

So is your government "Out to Get You?" perhaps not intentionally and probably not *you* specifically. But through their corruption, power grabs, ineptness and manipulation they're "getting" us all, and not in a good way. As *P.T. Barnum* once said "you can fool some of the people all of the time, and all of the people some of the time, but you can't fool all of the people all of the time!" Our government leaders would do well to remember this. The current level of deception and mistrust can't be good, and it won't end well.

As an illustration, I mentioned to a smart and active eighty-year-old fellow exercise regular at the beach, that I was writing a new book titled "Out To Get You." I explained it was about our Government and politics in America. Her reaction was immediate and not completely surprising. "Good," she said. "I'm glad." "We all feel that way!"

While I was finalizing the book for a September, 2013 release date an incredible thing happened. Congress balked at passing a budget for the following fiscal year and would not pass a *Continuing Resolution* to keep funding levels in place. The battle centered on a sore spot with the Tea Party *Republican* faction in the House of Representatives— *"Obamacare."* The House *Republicans* wanted to defund the new healthcare program and/or delay it, although their real goal was to eliminate it.

The *Affordable Healthcare Act* was *President Obama*'s signature accomplishment. He clearly didn't want to see it dismantled. So the game of "chicken" began between the Legislative and Executive branches of your Government. Both sides were intransigent. Political processes ground to a halt and the government experienced a partial shutdown. The political mainstays of negotiation and compromise were abandoned.

The chaos surrounding these events was too good to pass up. It was like "icing on the cake" for my book! Here I was writing a book about a dysfunctional government that's *Out to Get You* and there was a huge demonstration of this premise playing out before our very eyes.

Of course the events of late September into mid-October, 2013 were just another instance of the legendary ineptness of our leaders and their predilection for playing games. It also exemplified how viciously they were prepared to play.

During the "shutdown" examples of the tyranny of big government were too numerous to list. The *WWII Memorial* was closed to elderly veterans arriving in *Washington, D.C.* on "Honor Flights." *Park Service* officers prevented citizens from visiting landmarks like *Mount Rushmore, the Statue of Liberty, the Grand Canyon, and Florida Everglades.* Handles were removed from drinking fountains along jogging trails in the nation's capitol. *National Institutes of Health* drug trials for children with cancer were halted; military commissaries closed, sports broadcasts to active military suspended, and death benefits for soldiers killed in action delayed. But of course the shutdown did not close the Presidential retreat at *Camp David*, furlough the White House chefs, or shutter the Congressional gymnasium. No, the pain was not evenly spread as the mean-spirited, superior status and arrogant attitudes of the ruling class were in clear evidence.

The stakes were raised further when the Debt Ceiling came into play and the spectre of an unprecedented national default was at play. As I mentioned, this was too good an example to pass up so publication was delayed until the matter was "resolved" and I could include these events in this book.

You probably won't agree with everything I have written in this book and I would be disappointed if you did! We all have our unique viewpoints. What's important is to investigate, debate, discuss and critically analyze our government's policies, actions and performance rather than complacently accept what's happening or blindly follow party politics and political hyperbole.

Your government has become a "trickster." They constantly play tricks on us believing that we're too stupid or lazy to discover them or do anything about it. In this book we'll look at some of those tricks, who and what is behind them, what the consequences are, and how we can stop them.

Everything is changing.
People are taking their comedians seriously
and the politicians as a joke.

--Will Rogers

Suppose you were an idiot, and suppose you were a
member of Congress. But I repeat myself.

--Mark Twain

If 'pro' is the opposite of 'con'
what is the opposite of 'progress'?

--Paul Harvey

Chapter One

Out to Get You!

I've watched enough *"Matlock"* and *"Perry Mason"* reruns to know that one of the first things both the defense attorneys and the prosecutors look for is "motive." And crimes, unlike civil offenses are considered offenses against society itself. "Some crimes are more offensive than others precisely because of whom they victimize." (*Stephen McLeod*, Assistant D.A., *Kings Co.*, NY).

To continue with the legal analogy/model it follows then, if the Government is really out to get you, what could be their motive? In legal matters, particularly criminal cases, there are distinctions between Act, Intent, and Motive. And, to proceed with our analogy, if the Government "gets you" (in some harmful or malicious way) there is the <u>Act</u> of "getting you;" the <u>Intent</u> refers to their "state of mind" in this process, and their <u>Motive</u> would be the underlying reason for committing the act (of getting you).

Motives

The top five motives in criminal cases are: Rational Choice, Environment, Passion, Mental Illness, and Drug Addiction.

Although any of these could apply in the case of our government, the first two are most likely and worth exploring.

Rational Choice would include such specific reasons as: Financial Gain, Revenge, Opportunity, Neutralizing Opposition, or other Advantage.

Environment would suggest that the offense could be considered a normalized aspect of everyday life. There is a social learning element here and if the behavior is typical, condoned or promoted within the environment, it could be considered acceptable. We've all heard of high crime neighborhoods and the government may be one. For example if deception and corruption are typical behaviors they will likely be practiced by many members of the group. Could this be the case in Congress, some states and cities?

Is our Government Really "Out To Get You?"

Perhaps I'm just being paranoid. Maybe our Government isn't out to "get us" at all. I could be overly suspicious or hyper-vigilant or have some mental condition. Maybe the bad things are happening to our citizens and country are coincidental or a part of the "natural order of things." Probably our leaders have my interests at heart - yours too! - and are trying their best to make our lives better. But I don't think so. And after reading this book I believe you'll agree. The Government really is "Out to get You."

As I sought preliminary confirmation of my suspicions one resource I decided to use is the *Urban Dictionary*.

This dictionary has definitions for over seven million words and terms, but more importantly it isn't like traditional, staid, conservative dictionaries that use the least controversial and most literal definitions. The *Urban Dictionary* goes beyond strict definitions by including slang and cultural words or phrases in the context of contemporary usage, values and descriptions. It is particularly relevant to the younger generation and those who seek to understand them.

Definition of Paranoia:

"Believing that everyone is *out to get you*. Although it is true that everyone IS *out to get you*, such as the government and stalkers."

-from the *Urban Dictionary*

It's interesting and enlightening that in elaborating on the paranoid's belief that everyone is out to get them, the dictionary uses two examples: 1) the government, and 2) stalkers. And while this may make for amusing reading there is an element of truth. Stalkers we would agree are definitely a valid concern. And obviously people other than myself and my friend at the beach, think the Government is too. (At a minimum the contributors and editors at the on-line *Urban Dictionary*.) But a few words on a pop culture dictionary page don't prove anything. We'll have to make our case.

Most recent Presidents have been quite tricky. However, I only know of one who was publically labeled as tricky. That would be *Richard Milhous Nixon*, aka "Tricky Dick." But since then we've seen many more tricky administrations. After Tricky Dick, we saw Tricky Gerry, then Tricky Jimmy, Tricky Ron, Tricky George I and II, with Tricky Bill sandwiched between the father and son Bush's, and finally Tricky Barack.

Most of the tricks involved the economy, elections, espionage and spying, armed conflicts and war, ethical violations, legal difficulties (perjury, contempt of court), *IRS*, etc. Many scandals involved presidential appointees. Tricks seldom resulted in censure or legal difficulties, most skirted the law, were hidden or suppressed, or explained away. Some tricks may have actually resulted in positive outcomes such as *Reagan*'s tricking the Soviets into believing in the "Star Wars" nuclear defense shield (*Strategic Defense Initiative*).

Now let's get something else clear. My message is less accusatory and more exploratory. I'm not accusing the government of being a criminal enterprise or politicians of being criminals, although we all know of cases where that's been true.

You see, instead of being blatantly "criminalistic" our leaders are generally far more subtle, evasive and manipulative. As we'll see in the following chapters, I like to refer to them as "tricksters" but not in an innocent or playful sense.

Chapter Two

Your Government is a Trickster

Your government tricked you! Tricked you into believing that they have the power, and you do not. Tricked you into thinking that they can solve your problems. That they can provide you with rights, economic and social benefits and security. That they can make you safe and content. That by expanding their size, scope and influence you will be better off. That you enjoy the most freedoms and highest standard of living of any country in the world. And, they've tricked you in many other ways. We will cover several of the most prevalent tricks in this book, and explain the rationale behind them.

Tricks often involve sleight of hand or illusion, or jokes of some kind, but when the Government plays tricks, they're usually elaborate ones, believable ones, and on a large scale. Perhaps you've seen some of the great contemporary illusionists like *David Copperfield* or *David Blaine*. They're fantastic at making you believe you saw (or didn't see) something. *David Copperfield* even made the *Statue of Liberty* "disappear." (Something our politicians seem to be regularly trying to accomplish as well.) "Seeing is believing," they say. But we know from experience that's not always the case, particularly when tricks, illusion and deception are involved.

Before we go any further, though, I believe in defining terms. Therefore, on the next page you'll find a mainstream dictionary definition of
"trick," and "trickster." The definition is included in its entirety although only certain portions are most relevant.

Definition of *TRICK (from Merriam-Webster Dictionary)*

1
a : a crafty procedure or practice meant to deceive or defraud
b : a mischievous act : <u>prank</u>
c : an indiscreet or childish action
d : a deceptive, dexterous, or ingenious feat; *especially* : one designed to puzzle or amuse <a juggler's *tricks*>
2
a : a habitual peculiarity of behavior or manner <a horse with the *trick* of shying>
b : a characteristic and identifying feature <a *trick* of speech>
c : a delusive appearance especially when caused by art or legerdemain : an optical illusion <a mere *trick* of the light>
3
a (1) : a quick or artful way of getting a result : <u>knack</u> <the *trick* is to make it look natural> *(2)* : an instance of getting a desired result <one small adjustment will do the *trick*>
b : a technical device (as of an art or craft) <the *tricks* of stage technique>
4
: the cards played in one round of a card game often used as a scoring unit
5
a : a turn of duty at the helm usually lasting for two hours
b : <u>shift</u> 4b(1)
c : a trip taken as part of one's employment
d : a sexual act performed by a prostitute <turning *tricks*>; *also* : <u>john</u> 2
6
: an attractive child or woman <a cute little *trick*>

Definition of *TRICKSTER*

: one who <u>tricks</u>: as
a : a dishonest person who defrauds others by <u>trickery</u>
b : a person (as a stage magician) skilled in the use of tricks and illusion
c : a cunning or deceptive character appearing in various forms in the folklore of many cultures

Tricksters, that's what they are

How can they continue to trick a nation filled with bright, well-educated people? Well, if you spent *all* your time trying to deceive and manipulate people and persuade them to your way of thinking and garner their support you'd get pretty good at it too. Besides, we may be smart, but we're typically not well educated in the structure and workings of our government. Partially, this is by design. Most civics or government classes have been eliminated or dumbed down in the public school curricula. And, unless you're a Political Science major you probably won't, or didn't, encounter this education in college either. This suits the politicians just fine.

The *Center for Civic Education* reports that until the 1960's students generally received up to three civics courses. Currently, most students receive none and less than a third of teachers report covering civics and government materials in *any* courses they instruct.

You see, the fantasy that has been created by these politicians is exactly the opposite of reality. *You hold the power.* The ultimate power in this country, and in almost every other country on the planet, rests with the people. Even in dictatorships and totalitarian nations the people have the power to "throw the rascals out." In some countries it's accomplished through resistance, revolt and bloodshed, whereas in most modern nations it's accomplished peacefully. Think about it. We've seen many changes throughout history and it continues. A recent example is the "Arab Spring" government overthrows throughout countries in the *Middle East*. Sometimes these coups work well, but most do not. One power-hungry repressive regime is replaced by another amid promises of reform, but the scoundrels too often prevail. It's human nature to believe that changing faces will change fortunes, and sometimes it does, although fundamental reform is usually what is called for.

Any government will attempt to convince you that you're better off with them in power. But power means control and the thought of being controlled by power-hungry politicians, bureaucrats and government officials is abhorrent to most people. However, governments are good at convincing us that we are more secure if they are protecting us from ourselves, each other and external threats. And to some extent it is true! Certainly we can't, as an individual, protect our borders, prevent military attack, stop terrorism, prevent disease, crime, etc. But neither can they! No, we will never live in a risk-free country. It then becomes a question of scope and economics. A compromise of tradeoffs.

How much of our personal treasure, power, freedom and civil liberties are we willing to sacrifice to permit the government to engage in efforts to reduce our personal risk? And in some predictable and perhaps unseen ways by doing this do we actually increase dangers to our financial sufficiency and personal autonomy? These are complicated questions, significant tradeoffs, and interesting philosophical puzzles.

In my view, and perhaps yours, I would rather assume more responsibility for my own life, security and happiness and cede less to the government. To a large degree I resent the intrusion into my personal life and independence. The government is not your daddy!

Of course I want government to provide services that are important or essential, which I cannot, or prefer not to, and will improve my life. But I also believe that the services should be provided as close as possible to the people receiving them. In other words, by municipal, county, or state agencies and employees whenever possible. It just makes sense, and it's usually more cost-effective.

A report by the *Tax Foundation* compared salaries in the public and private sector (next page). The public sector was further divided into state/local, federal and military. Updates were provided in the *Washington Post*.

Average Wages and Salaries

Private Sector: $44,027
State and Local Gov't: $40,785
Federal Gov't: $78,467
Military: $42,290

Source: taxfoundation.org/washingtonpost.com

It should be noted, and fairly common knowledge, that the complete compensation package for government employees is, in most cases exceptional. The retirement, education, vacation and sick leave, healthcare, investment options, etc. all add up. For example, the military site *goarmy* has calculated the annual total compensation package at $99,000 (mentioning that 60% of compensation is not included in the army pay rate). And *FactCheck.org* calculates average federal non-military total compensation at $123,049!

This data provides another reason to delegate fewer services to the federal government and retain as many essential services as possible at the local level. It costs less!

"Economies of scale" are a myth when it comes to government. Instead, it's *diseconomies* of scale and mega disproportionally increasing waste. (I've often thought government can waste millions at the local level, billions at the State level and trillions at the Federal level before it becomes truly scandalous.)

The added benefit to local services is that these employees are usually more accountable and responsive to the people they provide services to. You might even know them. They could be your neighbor. Of course the federal employee could be your neighbor as well, but in their professional capacity he or she's in a role ultimately accountable to remote, less accessible entities.

Some Perspective

Let's get this clear, I don't care about your political persuasion or affiliation. This book was not written for Conservatives or Liberals, *Democrats* or *Republicans*, Independents or *Libertarians*, *Socialists* or *Communists*. I'm not trying to convince you of anything, but I am concerned about our country and I suspect you are too. I do have some biases, however, and my point of view is pro-freedom, pro-capitalism, pro-democracy and pro-people.

Despite the title of this book I'm not paranoid, anti-government, a conspiracy theorist, or an ultra-conservative. I don't advocate overthrow of our government, at least not yet. But I do believe we're on the wrong track and overdue for substantive change and reform. Our government has become too self-serving, too detached from the average person's concerns, too oblivious to the perils which lie ahead.

Forces for government inefficiency have always been in place. I recall teaching a college course in "Organizational Theory." One of the principal concepts involved organizational performance. Essentially, the model requires placement of organizations along a continuum running from "Rational" on one end to "Political" on the other. The theory is that rational organizations base decisions on reason and logic, whereas Political organizations employ power and influence as their modus operandi. All organizations have a mix of both styles, however, government obviously employs the less reasoned, more politically based methods. Thus the name: politics. Politics and political operatives are completely immersed in power and influence. So much so that logic and reason may rarely be encountered. Only the voters, the media, the pundits, and information organizations can stir up this political stew. And unfortunately, they're either reluctant to get involved or a big part of the whole mess, with agendas of their own.

In this book I have purposefully focused primarily on the highest levels of government, the executive branch of the federal government, particularly the President, and the legislative branch - the Congress.

The reason for this is visibility and relatability for the majority of readers. Besides they're at the top of the "food chain" and are responsible for the most corruption and for creating or failing to solve the biggest problems confronting the nation.

Tricky Leadership

Our top leaders are symbolic. Symbolic of the extent of government problems, of the political misuse of power, and of the political process. Indeed, symbolic of the country! Everyone knows the President; he's highly visible. Of course he's only an employee of ours and someone we have entrusted with temporary leadership responsibilities. I certainly don't want to minimize the position, because the power is real and the transformational potential is there. However, to a great extent the president is also emblematic of a system gone haywire. We have a government that is out of control and generally not operating in your or my best interests. This is a long-standing problem, one that didn't happen overnight. It's so tempting, so addictive, to enjoy so much power and prestige. This far too frequently leads to arrogance and a detachment from the people these officials represent. As a public official it's easy to stop listening and to think you know best. This is dangerous for our so-called democracy. The republic cannot thrive in a non-representative environment. You probably agree we certainly don't presently have the most altruistic, patriotic and committed transformational leadership at any level of government. Let's see what we can do about that!

So now it's evident. Something you certainly suspected, and probably knew—your government is a trickster. Not a trickster in the benign sense of playing innocent jokes and pranks, but in the far more sinister and offensive mode of trying to deceive you, mislead you, fleece you, perhaps even harm you. Yes, they play *dirty* tricks! It's time we put a stop to it.

Chapter Three

How Are You Doing?

Before we get too far into this book let's take a quiz. Now don't roll your eyes and groan; it's not that type of quiz! You're not back in school and you won't be graded. It's not difficult-- there are no right or wrong answers. It's a self-assessment, basically an "attitude survey."

It's essential that we have a framework for discussion and a baseline from which to compare. Sure it's subjective. It's all about our feelings, attitudes and confidence anyway. Perhaps you haven't given a great deal of thought to basic questions about your country and our government. Hopefully, this informal quiz will cause you to think and consider the current state of your well-being, your country and our government.

This is important. So important the President is required to provide Congress and the public with a "State of the Union" report each year. Likewise, Governors offer a similar "State of the State" report. And local governments do their version of this traditional assessment. I've always thought it should include a "public sentiment" portion; with feedback to the politicians and their constituents so we can stay on track. But maybe they don't care how we feel or what we think. After all, it's their country not ours, isn't it? Well, they seem to behave that way more often than not! So if you're ready, turn the page and answer as truthfully as you can. "Yes" or "No," "True or False." Here we go.

The Quiz

Q. Compared with previous times in your life...

1. Are you better off financially?
2. Do you feel more secure?
3. Do you feel safer?
4. Do you believe you, personally, have greater opportunity?
5. Do you trust your government more?
6. Do you trust the political process more?
7. Do you trust your elected leaders more?
8. Do you believe you have greater freedom?
9. Do you enjoy more privacy?
10. Are you happier?
11. Do you have more time to enjoy life?
12. Are your friends, family and neighbors doing better?
13. Are you more confident in the country's leadership?
14. Are you confident your government cares about you?
15. Do you believe the country's headed in the right direction?
16. Do you think foreign nations respect America more?
17. Are you confident America has a bright future?
18. Do you believe America is "the land of opportunity"?
19. Are you pleased with your community's services and finances?
20. Are you proud to be an American?

How was it? Pretty easy? Or did it make you think, perhaps in an uncomfortable sort of way?

You see, I suspect you're not as overjoyed with the "state of the union" as you may have once been. In fact, in a 2011 *Gallup* Survey only 11% reported satisfaction with the way things are going.

This widespread state of disaffection and dissatisfaction contributes to a sense of national malaise, a feeling that we individually might experience when we're ill or about to get sick? And, if our nation were a person, feeling this poorly would mean we are sick.

Sick in the head, the heart, the gut. Sick in the economy, leadership, foreign affairs, education, etc. Even sick in healthcare!

The diagnosis is in—we're ill, and in need of treatment. The course of treatment may be painful and prolonged. Fortunately our nation's founders outlined a prescription and set of rules for staying healthy and strong. But we ignored their good advice, and now we'll pay the price! Unless of course we enter into treatment and recovery mode.

Next we'll examine our nation's major ailments and presenting symptoms and complaints. Then we'll look at how, through a series of tricks, and deceptions, we got to this state.

OUT TO GET YOU

That government is best which governs least.

-Henry David Thoreau

The best minds are not in government.
If any were, business would steal them away.

--Ronald Reagan

In politics, nothing happens by accident. If it happens,
you can bet it was planned that way.

--Franklin D. Roosevelt

When the people fear the government, there is tyranny.
When the government fears the people, there is liberty.

--Thomas Jefferson

I am a radical in thought (and principle) and a con-
servative in method (and conduct).

--Rutherford B. Hayes

[32]

Chapter Four

The Biggest Issues

In chapter three you gained a general assessment of how satisfied you are with your current life situation as compared with past periods. How much of this can be attributed to the government's actions and policies? As it turns out, quite a bit.

What do your friends, neighbors, and other Americans believe are the Nation's biggest problems? The *Gallup* organization has conducted surveys to determine this very thing for a number of years. In *Gallup's* July, 2013 study economic issues ranked, as they always do, at the top, although sub-issues within that general category and non-economic issues were also ranked. Here are the top concerns:

Economic Issues:
Economy in General
Unemployment
Federal Budget
Lack of money
Taxes
Non-economic issues:
Dissatisfaction with government
Healthcare
Ethics/Morality
Immigration/illegal aliens
Education

Of course with our diverse population the range of priority issues is quite broad and many others are identified. For example other less visible concerns in the economic category include: Fuel prices, cost of living/inflation, corporate corruption, taxes, gap between rich and poor, wages, recession, foreign trade/trade deficit, etc. And in the non-economic area: Judicial system (courts/laws), foreign aid, crime/violence, hunger/homelessness, war/fear of war, lack of respect, gun control, welfare, race relations, national security, terrorism, gay rights, abortion, military defense, drugs, social security, technology, media, elections...

You certainly have your own "hot button" issues, and major concerns, and I suspect we will be examining several of them. You may even discover a few that are more important to you than you previously re-alized, but all of the topics included are problems and priorities for the country. By design and necessity the book does not examine every issue in depth. A survey approach has been taken covering a variety of topics. Should you want to go deeply into any area on the list in this chapter or throughout the book, perhaps some topic close to your heart, you may choose to do further research. And if you do there are excellent single subject books you can read which cover each of the major problems and several of the less conspicuous ones, exclusively and in detail.

In the next chapter we will discuss the biggest problem, and the most important issue for most Americans—the ECONOMY.

Chapter Five

The Economic Trick

The economic trick is massive in scale and is motivated by greed. Your government is in bed with the wealthiest corporations and individuals in the country. They try to make you believe they're concerned about your plight, while deceiving you about their intent. Their intent is to make themselves, their friends and supporters wealthier at your expense.

The cruelest trick of all may be the economic trick. The American Dream was primarily an economic one. This "dream," for decades involved a good paying job, a home, an automobile and an economically secure family. It was a dream of freedom, success, prosperity and social mobility. An essential component of the dream was progress through effort, i.e., "hard work." The work ethic and the dream ethos were inextricably linked. America was viewed as a country where everyone, without regard to class or race, could succeed providing they were willing to put in the work, discipline and sacrifice. Now in all fairness we will note that this ideal was never completely realized although it was substantially true for many Americans for much of our history. All this has changed.

According to an *Associated Press* report on July 28, 2013: "Four out of 5 U.S. adults struggle with joblessness, near poverty or reliance on welfare for at least parts of their lives, a sign of deteriorating economic security and an elusive American dream."

The study defines "economic insecurity" as a year or more of periodic joblessness, reliance on government aid such as food stamps (now *SNAP*) or income below 150 percent of the poverty line.

What happened? Eighty percent of Americans in financial trouble? The researchers cite: "[an] increasingly globalized U.S. economy, the widening gap between rich and poor and loss of good-paying manu-facturing jobs" as reasons for the trend.

Furthermore, economic insecurity has become an equal opportunity condition with non-minorities being the fastest growing segment of sufferers. President *Barack Obama* in mid-2013 began to renew his administration's emphasis on improving the economy, saying in sever-al speeches that his highest priority is to "rebuild ladders of opportunity" and reverse income inequality. One would think that this would have been a top priority all along, particularly with the seem-ingly never-ending Great Recession which most observers agree began in 2008.

Do our lawmakers understand the importance of this problem and the implicit danger to the delicate social balance in our society? Probably not. They live in a different society. A society of privilege and wealth. The huge gap between the richest and poorest in our society is every bit as disturbing as the huge division between rich and poor in underdeveloped nations. Perhaps more disturbing, because we've been accustomed to a more equal, less dramatically skewed differences.

The worlds of the rich and the poor seldom intersect, but could collide! Just as most Americans don't know much about the inhabitants of *New Guinea*, most residents of *Beverly Hills* don't know much about the people in *Compton*. We tend to associate with our friends and the people in our neighborhood. When I lived in *Los Angeles* I lived in the hills. It was great to have a view and privacy, but those of us who lived at the hilltop had to drive through the poorer neighborhoods in order to travel to our homes. Income stratification by elevation, you could call it.

Although the workplace may have a little more economic diversity than our neighborhood there's also a hierarchy in effect, and besides people typically exhibit different behaviors at work. Your immediate community is also generally pretty homogeneous, no matter where you live. Of course you may shop at the mall, or go to the movie theatre but our interactions with others at those venues is more scripted and less interactive.

As I learned in a Sociology class, prejudice arises from ignorance and fear. That phenomenon is not limited to racial prejudice, it also applies to class differences. America was supposed to be a classless society without an aristocracy, royalty or caste system. For years we seemed to be moving that direction, but recently I hear the uncomfortable rumbling of "class war."

The Housing Bubble

Because of its scope and impact the government sponsored housing bubble deserves special, more extensive treatment. One of the largest, most destructive tricks in history is the housing boom, ensuing crash, and aftermath. Beginning in 1992 and continuing into the early twenty-first century the U.S. government sponsored and promoted an unprecedented housing boom. In that year Congress acted to require the two government mega housing agencies commonly known as *Fannie Mae* and *Freddie Mac* to engage in an affordable housing program. Then in 1995 Congress, under the *Community Reinvestment Act*, required banks to provide home loans to "underserved communities," including a provision to offer loans to home buyers with poor credit who could not qualify for conventional loans. Requirements continued to be eased to include: zero down payment, low down, variable interest rates, negative amortization, liberal or no income documentation, etc. This government sponsored home-ownership expansion initially involved a trillion-dollar commitment and eventually much, much more. The program was so successful that at one point 40% of the mortgages were sub-prime-- 25 million loans! As we all now know, the government and the banks were flooded with loans of questionable quality.

Wall Street stepped up to "repackage" loans into Mortgage Backed Securities with a higher (blended) credit rating. These credit instruments were then sold to investors all over the world.

When the loans began going sour (partially as a consequence of higher unemployment beginning in 2006) the extent of the problem was revealed and the housing crash, Great Recession, and world-wide credit crisis began to unfold. At the apex of the crisis banks refused to loan to each other or customers knowing the poor quality and consequent risk of assets financial institutions were holding.

The untold human suffering, financial ruin, economic stagnation and ruined futures can be directly traced to the government's policies and actions. When asked about the crisis, *Barney Frank* who was the Chair of the *House Financial Services Committee* admitted that "it was a mistake to force home ownership on people who couldn't afford it." He went on to say: "…they would have been better off renting." Three Presidents supported these careless and destructive policies: *Clinton*, *Bush*, and *Obama*. Once again, your government in action with misguided social and economic reengineering projects gone horribly awry.

Of course the trick worked. The politicians gained votes, the economy boomed (especially builders, lenders, and Wall Street), people gained wealth as property values increased then the bubble burst and the housing and mortgage markets collapsed. Then the homeowners lost money, the banks did too, the bailouts came, the banks made money, so did Wall Street, the government got praise. What a joke.

The Government Pension Bubble

As if the Housing Bubble, the Credit Bubble, the Student Loan Bubble, and the Debt Crisis were not enough, Federal, State and Local governments have promised trillions of dollars in retirement and healthcare benefits to their employees. Money that they don't have.

[39]

And these are generous benefits when compared with private sector pensions which are usually based on 401k plans that the employee funds with perhaps some nominal "matching" employer contribution.

In 2010 the only state with a fully-funded pension program was *Wisconsin*. The worst were *Connecticut, Illinois, Kentucky* and *Rhode Island* with less than 55% of their obligations funded. *Government Accounting Standards* require at least 80% dedicated funding for a plan to rate as "healthy." The estimated state and local pension shortfall is $1.3 trillion!

A 2012 article in *USA Today* reported that 21,000 federal retirees received pensions exceeding $100,000 annually. *DEA* (Drug Enforcement), *IRS, FBI*, and *SSA* (Social Security Administration) retirees comprised the largest numbers of those with the highest pensions. In 1986 Congress replaced the Federal employees with a less costly one that combined a less generous defined-benefit component with an at-risk 401K.

The pension fund is a convenient piggy bank for government. In the Federal Budget crisis the government borrowed money to tide them over. Not a good practice as we learned from *Social Security*. And the federal employee pension fund has an estimated $2 trillion unfunded liability. Military pensions are particularly worrisome because our warriors are eligible for 50% of their salary after only twenty years' service, meaning that retirees would often receive monthly government stipends for most of their life. For example, a soldier who joined the service at age 18 could theoretically retire at the youthful age of 38! Should he or she live an average life span they would be retired twice as long as they worked! And because of cost-of-living escalators would receive pensions which represent multiples of their earned wages. With typical *COLA*s a retiree could, over a lifetime, easily double or triple their highest active duty monthly pay. The unfunded liability for military pensions is estimated to top $5.7 trillion in 2034 according to a 2012 article in *Pensions and Investments*.

Pension promising and pension spiking is a great political trick and gains the support and votes of many public employees.

I saved the best pension plan of all for last: *The Congressional Pension Plan*. Members of Congress are eligible for their pension at 62 years of age after serving only five years or at age 50 after twenty. Retired Congressional members of the *Civil Service Retirement System* received an average of $71,472 in 2012 according to the *Congressional Research Service*. Their gracious retirement after perhaps only a few years is an excellent trick.

The Federal Budget

The federal budget is enormous and not well understood. Interestingly there is little discretion in most expenditure areas because of earmarks for programs and functions. As you will see, almost all of the money is gobbled up by a few major programs/expenditure categories. The Chart on the following page shows how your government spends your money.

As you will note the big four categories are: *Interest on the debt, Defense, Health and Human Services* (primarily healthcare), and *Social Security*. The least disturbing of these high-ticket expenditures is *Social Security* as it serves a particularly important social purpose and has its own contributory-based funding scheme. Of course we've all heard about the future solvency of *Social Security* which according to a *CBO* analysis experienced in 2010, for the first time, expenditures which exceeded revenues. And the gap continues to grow. Under current law the Disability portion will be exhausted in 2013 and the Old Age Security component in 2038. To extend the fiscal viability of the program some analysts recommend eliminating the contribution ceiling ($113,700 in 2013) and taxing all earned income.

[41]

The *Medicare* and *Medicaid* programs also have imminent solvency issues. For *Medicare*'s HI (Hospital Insurance program) there has not been an income limitation on employee or employer contributions since 1993.

The most problematic budget item is interest on the national debt. Interest paid which funds no services or programs directly but is used as a stopgap measure to allow continuation of overall spending levels and an artificial means to balance the budget. This huge expenditure merely siphons money from the budget to pay back fiscally irresponsible prior and projected overspending and commitments. It also encourages legislators to continue "fantasy" budgets, authorize new and expanded commitments, and avoid responsibly. In time it could result in major inflationary pressures.

It should be obvious that our government spends enormous, almost inconceivable amounts of money on such a wide array of programs that almost everyone's life is impacted to some degree. And hidden within the general categories, are thousands of smaller programs and initiatives which probably no single individual is completely aware of or familiar with.

Now take a close look, on the next page, at how our Government spends your money. Be sure to notice the scale on the horizontal axis of the bar chart – it is measured in billions of dollars with markers at each $100 billion increment!

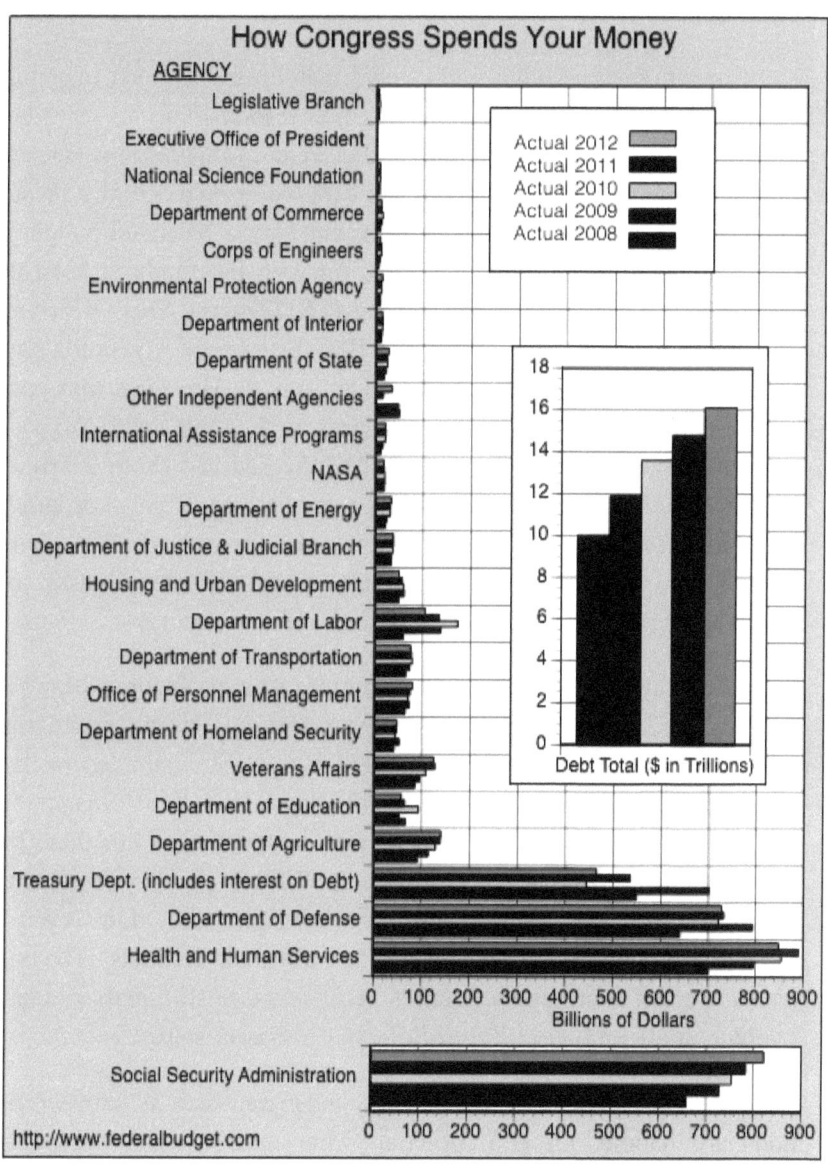

The Fed

The *Federal Reserve Bank,* and its chairman have the power to control the money supply of the country. It's their responsibility to set monetary policy including interest rates and currency valuation, oversee and lend to member institutions and make sure we're on a sound fiduciary footing. But with continuing deficits and nary a balanced budget in sight, the *Fed* has to somehow come up with the funds to keep the country going. They do this by selling *U.S. Treasury Notes* which are primary obligations of the nation. But they frequently don't have enough customers, so they buy some themselves. However, they can't buy them directly so they make purchases on the open market in competition with other entities. In mid-2012 the Fed had about 2 Trillion Dollars' worth of Treasury Notes. (For comparison, China, our largest client for these instruments has about the same amount [$2T]). Sometimes I think they may have lost their minds with this circular and risky approach to funding our continuing over-expending!

Let me explain: As a nation we spend more than our income allows so we have to go into debt. We borrow money by issuing promissory notes. However, not enough customers want to buy them, so we buy them ourselves. Then we print money out of thin-air to finance our purchases. Insanity or what? If a private company tried this the officers would be thrown in jail (ala *Enron*). Why does the world put up with this? Because, such as the case with *China,* they don't want to see us go broke because then we couldn't buy their products. The only reason we can continue the scam is because we're still, perhaps tentatively, holding onto our *"World Reserve Currency"* status.

Since we have the Reserve Currency, most transactions between nations are handled in U.S. dollars. Other nations don't enjoy this advantage and they're envious. They're also concerned that we might be running a giant *Ponzi* scheme. The game can't go on indefinitely, and one day it will all come crashing down. Unless, of course, we bite the fiscal bullet, and attempt to balance our budget.

[44]

Which is unlikely because the economy, propped up by this fantasy money, would probably go into a tailspin. Fed Chairman *Ben Bernanke* is a scholarly man and a student of the Great Depression. As this book was about to be published the *Fed* (9/18/13) announced continuation of the "stimulus," meaning they will continue to pump $85 billion a month into the economy. It's like a "crack-addict" thinking the solution to his problem is more drugs.

The *Fed* Chairman is affectionately known as "Helicopter Ben" as a result of a comment that he would prefer to see the *Fed* use helicopters to drop money from the sky if this would avoid another Depression. *President Obama* has nominated *Janet Yellen*, Assistant Fed Chair and an economist with similar policy views to succeed *Bernanke* when his term ends in 2014.

Recovery Propaganda

How many times have you heard the economy is in recovery? And, how many times have you believed it? This isn't a real recovery! It's an artificial one. Without the continued infusion of freshly printed money to keep the patient (U.S. economy) alive, we would still be going backwards. The Government created the Great Recession and the government has (with the intervention of the Fed) created a not-so-great recovery. The Government propaganda machine regularly announces that the economy is in recovery mode. A jobless recovery, but a recovery nonetheless. They must do this of course, because our increasingly consumer and service-dominated economy requires it. A recovery demands confidence, so you and I will go out and spend. Some administrations are more subtle than others in this regard. Perhaps the most blatant attempt at stimulating consumerism was the speech given by President *George W. Bush* just two weeks after 9/11. He encouraged the American public to "go shopping." Even more specifically: "Go down to Disney World in Florida. Take your families and enjoy life…"

Financial Inequality

America has another money problem. It's an unequal distribution of wealth. Not just a minor maldistribution but a grotesquely exaggerated one. You see the middle class thinks they have money -- in reality they're poor. And the poor, well, they exist in desperation city! The concentration of wealth in the hands of so few would make *Marie Antoinette* blush. The rich in the *United States* are so rich the extent of their wealth is incomprehensible to all but a few. In fact just 400 *Americans*, the richest, have about the same combined wealth as half of *all Americans* and the poorest 80% have only 7% of the wealth. That astounding statistic bears repeating, the bottom 80% have only 7%! (Verified source *Economic Journal*: via Alan Grayson, D-FL.)

The distribution of wealth in this country following WWII was shaped like a "football," fat in the middle and tapered on the ends. Then in the 1990's it began to look more like a pear with many less in the middle (class) a little bulge at the top, and significantly more people at the bottom. Now its beginning to look more like a dumbbell turned on end; big on both ends and skinny in the middle, reflecting continued growth of the upper and lower classes and further erosion of the middle-class.

As I was putting the "finishing touches" on this book I came across an article describing former Labor Secretary *Robert Reich*'s new documentary *"Inequality for All"* lamenting the fact that instead of economic progress we've seen continuing deterioration. *Reich* states that wealth inequality in this country is now greater than it was prior to the Great Depression; an ominous indicator.

Despite the income inequality problem - and it's a real one - income mobility may be an even more important consideration. We've all heard the saying "the rich get richer," and perhaps we've heard its corollary too -- "the poor get poorer." But is it true? Twenty to forty percent of Americans shift between income quartiles over a five year period.

This movement supports the premise that opportunity is still present in our economy. It may be more difficult, but individuals are still moving up the economic ladder. And, unfortunately others are moving down. In recent years the numbers moving up have shrunk. But don't think the statistics apply directly to you or your opportunity. It just doesn't work that way. No matter how much the government stacks the deck against you, your potential and determination can prevail.

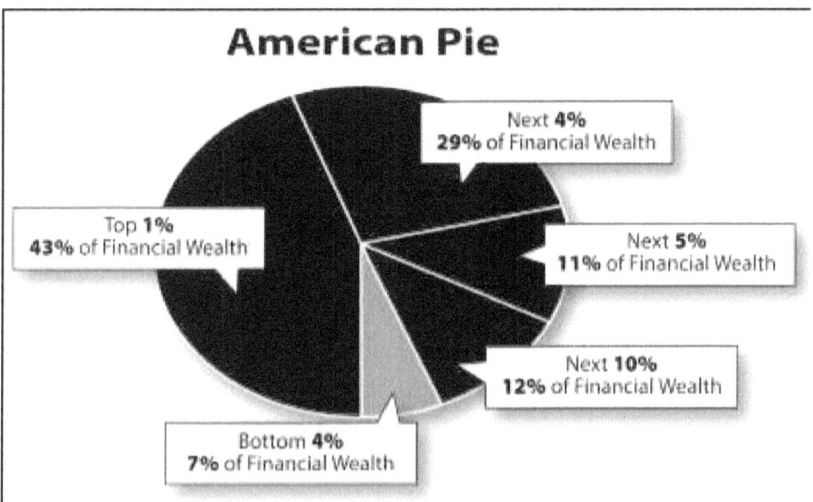

American Pie

Next **4%**
29% of Financial Wealth

Top **1%**
43% of Financial Wealth

Next **5%**
11% of Financial Wealth

Next **10%**
12% of Financial Wealth

Bottom **4%**
7% of Financial Wealth

Adapted from Wolff, E. N. (2010). **Recent trends in household wealth in the United States: Rising debt and the middle-class squeeze - an update to 2007**. *Working Paper No. 589*. Annadale-on-Hudson, NY: The Levy Economics Institute of Bard College.

Incidentally, the American pie continues to be cut more in favor of the rich. Near the end of 2013, only 400 hundred households get to eat about half of it. It's a really tasty pie, too, because the only ingredient is money. How big is your slice? A satisfying portion or a tiny sliver?

How does the U.S. Compare?

Not only is this inequality enormous; it places us near the top of world-wide inequality. Only four countries have a more unequal distribution than us. We rank fifth, right behind *Denmark, Namibia, Switzerland and Zimbabwe*.

The calculation method used is the *Gini Coefficient*, a standardized means of comparison. However, when this methodology is used to compare *income* instead of *wealth* a quite different picture emerges. In terms of income inequality, the U.S. ranks somewhere near the middle.

The total picture then is while a few people hold much of the nation's wealth they don't enjoy such an incredible advantage in annual income. The explanation for this phenomenon is actually quite simple. Huge fortunes have been amassed in this country as a result of a capitalistic system and much of this wealth has remained in those same hands, then passed down through family generations. Think of the *Rockefeller's*, the *Koch's*, the *Walton's*, the *DuPont's*, and the *Mars* families. Several dynasties have fallen from the wealth apex, however, such as the *Carnegie's* (philanthropy), *Ford's* (stock decline), and the *Kennedy's* (multiple reasons). Also, the two richest individuals in the country at this time, *Bill Gates* and *Warren Buffet* are busy giving away most of their fortunes through charitable endeavors.

Bottom line, there is a lot of money concentrated at the top in our society. The government has exacerbated this problem through tax rules that limit total tax burden and treat passive (investment) income more favorably than earned (wage) income, and through gross mismanagement of the economy, bailouts, inappropriately favored industries, de-industrialization, globalization, etc.

I believe in a society that offers incentives for entrepreneurship and business acumen. Opportunity to succeed and be rewarded for your ideas, talent and effort is a positive feature of the capitalistic model.

Of course an increase in economic inclusiveness is essential and needs to be a priority. Otherwise the "class wars" that people talk about might become an unpleasant reality.

Spending Priorities

What would your spending priorities be? Would they match the existing ones? Or would you prefer to see some reduced or eliminated and others, perhaps, increased? Do you think we spend too much on defense? Should we spend more on the *National Science Foundation*? How about education? Whatever your priorities it would take detailed knowledge and investigation to make an informed decision. The numbers are so big and the structure and detail so confusing that the average person just blanks out. This is where the *CBO* (Congressional Budget Office) comes in. They were created to help Congress, and the public objectively understand the fiscal consequences of their decisions before programs are enacted into law.

How long do you think our government can continue spending more than its income? A short time, a long time, perhaps forever? And what should be done about it? Obviously, just as with your household budget, balance can be achieved by reducing expenses or increasing income, or some combination of the two. A policy of growing the real economy, expanding the private sector and increased participation of the workforce would help immensely. We're in a different time period and our strategies must adapt. It's not like the period following WWII when we were the only major industrial economy with our productive capacity left intact. Everyone needed to buy our products and they did, all over the world. That condition supported our domestic consumption and fueled huge amounts of exports for much of the second half of the twentieth century.

We need a contemporary strategy, one aimed at succeeding in the increasingly competitive international market. New, forward-thinking ideas and programs instead of deadlocks, immobilization and excuses.

We can't afford to waste a generation of minds and talent in dead-end jobs with marginal pay scales. We owe it to them to revitalize the American Dream. It seems a national economic initiative is in order. Not modeled on the post-depression *New Deal* or *WPA*, but one more suited to the current environment and its challenges, and one that has the private sector at its core.

Simplistic strategies such as raising the minimum wage won't do. Over the short term that often has the effect of reducing employment and spiking inflation while not addressing the root cause. New and better jobs are required; ones with a future.

The Sequester

The boldest budgetary action taken by Congress and approved by the President in recent years has been the *sequester* (a general cut in government spending). Incidentally, the White House website defines the term differently than *Webster*. Their (clearly politicized) definition: *"Harmful automatic budget cuts — known as the sequester — threaten hundreds of thousands of jobs, and cut vital services for children, seniors, people with mental illness and our men and women in uniform"*.

The *sequester* occurred by happenstance, almost inadvertence, the result of an agreement between *President Obama* and Speaker of the House *John Boehner* in 2011. The result: After budget increases for many years, federal expenditures have actually decreased recently. Remember the horror story warnings from politicians? Airplanes would crash, national parks would close, passports wouldn't be issued, The President never thought the sequester would actually happen as he inadvertently constrained his ability to increase expenditures due to this federal debt cap, triggered by slow economic growth.

So far Congress has resisted the temptation to break the *sequester* and yield to pressures to increase social spending. Federal agencies have had to contend with 2-5% cuts, and monthly furloughs of employees.

[50]

But what a surprise! It hasn't been as painful, and certainly nowhere near the disaster the politicians forecast. There's a lesson in this. A lesson that the government can learn, and the private sector already knows—sometimes you have to cut expenses, yet it can result in greater efficiencies and cost-effectiveness. What a novel concept.

The 2013 Budget Trick

Just as this book was about to be released for publication, all Hell broke loose. Political drama at its best. House *Republicans*, always opposed to *Obamacare*, decided to defund the program in their FY2014 budget extension bill. The Democratically controlled Senate, of course, rejected their proposal. Then the *Republicans,* to break the impasse, suggested a Conference Committee to resolve differences. The Senate rejected that idea as well, unless *Obamacare* funding was included at the outset. The midnight deadline on September 30th passed and October 1st arrived with no resolution; the Government prepared to shut down. The game of "chicken" and brinksmanship was over. Neither side won. The Government shut down and the Tea Party faction was intoxicated with their power to cause mischief and disruption. This was the first shutdown in seventeen years although there have been numerous events like this in recent history – lasting from one to 21 days.

A Government shutdown, like many things in *Washington* is not what you might think. Although the Government technically had no appro-priations for programs and services that didn't mean that everything stopped. Most services continued as always, the mail was delivered, healthcare was provided, air traffic controllers reported to work, the military continued their activities, law enforcement too.

All essential government functions were exempt from closure includ-ing Congress! In fact 83% of government employees continued working. However, federal parks and museums were closed, *NASA* was largely down and the *IRS* shut down (Hooray!).

The *Patent Office* was closed and federally backed home loans were suspended. Although there was not much impact for the average person.

The President regularly appeared on TV blaming the *Tea Party Republicans* for the shutdown. On October 1st he feigned outrage, saying: "One faction of one party in one house of Congress in one branch of government doesn't get to shut down the entire government just to re-fight the results of an election." Viewers thought he appeared to be genuinely concerned about the consequences for the nation. But it was all part of a game, a façade, a trick to find opportunity in crisis. Do you believe the President really wanted to see the problem resolved? No, there was political advantage at stake. Those *reckless Republicans* were at it again. Those Tea Partiers. Those Neanderthal politicians trying to deny Americans their right to healthcare. The name-calling and finger-pointing continued. The blame game was in full force. *Republicans* portraying *Obamacare* as a failure; an unaffordable boondoggle. *Democrats* claiming it was an essential program for the uninsured, and an important safety-net for all Americans. Meanwhile people were trying to sign up for the program as its funding sources were not impacted by the shutdown. The obligation was clear, the enrollees and participants were signing up. A massive new government entitlement program was beginning. (For more about *Obamacare* see Chapter Eight – The Healthcare Trick.)

The biggest event of October 2013 was yet to come. The day when the Federal Government was forecast to actually run out of money and have to raise the debt limit. That event was calculated to occur on October 17th and missing that deadline could have disastrous consequences. The U.S. would be in DEFAULT and could not pay its bills or creditors for the first time in history. It would surely result in another national credit downgrade and jeopardize the dollar's World Reserve Currency status.

President *Obama* was reminded of his remarks on the Senate floor just seven years earlier:

The fact that we are here today to debate raising America's debt limit is a sign of leadership failure. It is a sign that the US Government can not pay its own bills. It is a sign that we now depend on ongoing financial assistance from foreign countries to finance our Government's reckless fiscal policies. Increasing America's debt weakens us domestically and internationally. Leadership means that "the buck stops here." Instead, Washington is shifting the burden of bad choices today onto the backs of our children and grandchildren. America has a debt problem and a failure of leadership. Americans deserve better. (*Abridged from Congressional Record*)

Reminded that he had spoken those words before the Senate (on March 6, 2006), in a *Good Morning America* interview back in 2011 (4/15/11) *Obama* then said:

I think that it's important to understand the vantage point of a senator versus the vantage point of a president. When you're a senator, traditionally what's happened is, this is always a lousy vote. Nobody likes to be tagged as having increased the debt limit — for the United States by a trillion dollars. As president, you start realizing, you know what, we, we can't play around with this stuff. This is the full faith and credit of the United States. And so that was just an example of a new senator making what is a political vote as opposed to doing what was important for the country.

Oh how our words can come back to haunt us. Incidentally, although *Senator Obama* voted against the debt increase the resolution passed 58 to 42.

During the impasse the *House of Representatives* spent several days creating bills aimed at reopening parts of the government, but not *Obamacare*. The Senate would hear none of it. They demanded unrestricted continuing budget and debt ceiling resolutions; so called "Clean" *Continuing Resolutions* with no conditions (as opposed to the "dirty" resolutions excluding *Obamacare*). The *Speaker of the House*, *Senate Majority Leader* and *Treasury Secretary* became regulars on TV talk shows, but the stalemate went on. Like kids on a playground all major participants (Administration and Congress) were unwilling to compromise or negotiate; all they were prepared to do was fight and cry.

The worldwide media looked on with disbelief and amazement not understanding the nature of American political theatre.

[53]

Then, on October 7th *Chinese* officials warned the United States to resolve the [debt ceiling] issues and protect *China*'s investments. It was getting serious but did the trickster politicians understand the significance or were they too stubborn and arrogant? American voters, foreign leaders, business interests, our creditors and citizens the world over were laughing and shocked at the incompetence and recklessness of the world's preeminent superpower. However, unless our politicians were willing to compromise there was no end in sight. More importantly, I could not finish this book! Of course my opportunity in this particular crisis was the ability to include an excellent current example of "tricksterism," party politics, game-playing, media manipulation, and government dysfunctionality.

Ten days into the "shutdown" some progress began to appear. The *Republicans*, who had suffered the most in public opinion polls were invited to meet with *President Obama* and the *Democratic* leadership. Key members of both parties in both Congressional houses met at the White House. In anticipation of a deal, the stock market leaped, with the *Dow-Jones* Average gaining 323 points that day. It seemed as though some type of resolution was imminent. Besides, a three-day holiday (*Columbus* Day) weekend was coming up, and the Friday federal payday was the first one in which some federal employees would receive short-changed checks.

Everyone was tired of the uncertainty: the public, our foreign creditors, the politicians, the financial markets, etc. The world's top bankers issued dire warnings of catastrophe: Another recession, a credit collapse, a weakened dollar, and another credit downgrade for the USA. We were becoming an international laughingstock!

On Saturday, October 12th a computer glitch rendered the *EBT* (Electronics Benefit Transfer) system inoperable and beneficiaries thought it resulted from the government shutdown. It didn't, although people were already edgy and suspicious of the Government.

The bickering and posturing continued into a third week. On October 14th *China* warned us again, as did *International Monetary Fund* chief *Christine Lagarde*, saying there was "a risk of massive disruption the world over." Then on October 15th agreement was supposedly reached but the deal again fell through. Seventy percent were now blaming the *Republicans*. A day later and just a few hours before default an agreement was reached between the White House and the *Senate*. All that was left was to gain approval of both houses of Congress and the President would sign it into law. The deal would essentially kick the can down the road a few months. The political quagmire was so treacherous that that's all they could do. Later in the day both the *House* and the *Senate* agreed to reopen the Government until January 15, 2014 and extend the Government's borrowing authority until February 7 and the President signed the bill a few minutes after midnight. Secretly, the politicians had attached to the not-so-clean bill a number of new spending measures: $2.2 billion for a dam in Kentucky; $174,000 for the widow of one of the richest members of Congress; $450 million for flood rebuilding in Colorado; $600 million to fight wildfires; $1million for the Mine Safety Dept.; and, $2.1 million to a cyberintelligence watchdog group. They just can't help themselves!

Far from a solution the bill was a stopgap measure allowing the U.S. to continue functioning as a nation. Everyone celebrated the latest trick and we could all enjoy the Holiday Season. We were safe until the next crisis.

A Lost Generation?

A Recession for adults has been a Depression for teens. Although the unemployment rate is slowly dropping for adults it has increased significantly for teens. Plus, an important but little discussed element of unemployment is the "churn rate," the rate at which people leave one job and move to another. This churning of the workforce has slowed substantially.

The currently employed are staying with their employer(s) and significantly more reticent to switch jobs or careers, making it difficult for new entrants or transfers. Companies and government offices have also been cutting back on their commitment to student internships. As a result of all these factors summer jobs were scarce in 2013 with only one in three teens landing a job. For comparison, a decade ago (1999) 52% of young people had summertime work. Now it's only half that amount. The picture is even bleaker for racial minorities with only 19% of African-American teenagers working. Before you think this isn't that important, consider this: Teenagers with paid work experience graduate from college at a higher rate, and learn important social and employment skills and attitudes. They're also more likely to succeed in the workforce after graduation from college and gain valuable preparation for independence.

In today's economy large numbers of teenagers aren't even bothering to get a Driver's License. Young adults are also living at home longer, mostly for economic reasons. According to a *Wall Street Journal* article (Aug. 27, 2013) 13.6 percent of Americans aged 25 to 34 now live at home. And, because of the bad economy there's less stigma attached to living at home longer. Unfortunately there is less opportunity to leave and perhaps less incentive as well, as many of the jobs traditionally filled by teens are now occupied by adults.

Our Economic Future

Considering the aforementioned our future looks pretty dicey, if not downright bleak. There is, however, one exceptionally bright spot emerging on the economic horizon: Oil discovery and production on U.S. soil. After decades of dependence on foreign oil, primarily from *Middle Eastern* sources, the United States is once again flirting with oil independence. New technologies to free oil from shale rock formations by a "fracking" process are rapidly expanding domestic oil production. And, on July 10, 2013 *Bloomberg* reported the highest level of U.S. oil production in twenty years.

This "wild card" in the economic game could revitalize the economy and inject substantial revenue, while simultaneously reducing imports and overseas outflows of capital. It's a fascinating scenario, and the type of good fortune we could use. By itself this phenomenon will not "save the economy" even though it's a huge positive. We'll see. Hope for the best!

There is also a move to return manufacturing to this country. There are good reasons for that because foreign labor is becoming increasingly expensive as is transporting products to our shores. Combined with the fact that *American* employees are among the most productive in the world, makes this option even more attractive.

With a few positive trends occurring we may be able to stave off or reduce our rate of economic decline, but our government will need to be less greedy, more strategic, less corrupt, more patriotic, and definitely show greater support for the working and middle class.

You'll probably notice that I have spent more time on the economy than most of the other issues in this book. First, because it's the number one problem on almost everyone's list; and second because it's such an incredible mess.

From the 1930's to the 1980's average *American* income tripled with unemployment bottoming out at 4% in the 1960's. The percentage of *American*s owning automobiles and houses steadily increased. Wages soared, leisure time increased, benefits boomed, as did savings and investments. In 1980 *America* was ranked number 1 in standard of living among industrialized nations. (*OCED* reports) The good times lasted into the 1990's with the U.S. holding on to the top ranking. By the end of the first decade of the 21st century we had fallen some, but were still ranked in the top twenty. Countries with the highest standards of living include *Norway, Australia and Iceland*, and at the other end of the scale are *Niger, Afghanistan, and Sierra Leone*. The standard of living rankings include more than just income, but healthcare, diet, quality of life elements, etc.

It's not unrealistic for us to try and regain the number one position but the government will have to stop playing tricks and get down to *business*.

Can We Learn From Other Nations?

The economy du jour is *Germany*. Before that it was *China*. And, before that the U.S. and *Japan*. I remember 25 years ago when we were teaching the Japanese *Kaizen* (continuous improvement) model in college business courses. *Japan* was a dominant economy at that point and the U.S. was in the doldrums. Once again the U.S. economy is stagnant, but so is *Japan*, although both are turning up. Now *Germany* is a favorite. In many ways their economy is similar to ours. Of course theirs has greater government intervention and control.

Germany until recently was accused of having an obsolete, outdated model. Economists and business leaders are now looking toward *Germany* as perhaps having some features we would do well to emulate. For example according to a 2012 *Der Spiegel* article: *Germany* has a trade surplus of $120 billion euros, while the U.S. has a $423 billion deficit (expenditures exceeding revenue).

The U.S. loses 200,000 industrial jobs a year, and only 9% of Americans are now employed in factories and the manufacturing sector accounts for only 12% of *GDP*. In *Germany* manufacturing is 26% of *GDP*. Here we talk much about the small to mid-sized businesses being an "engine of growth." It's the same in *Germany* where these firms account for the "lion's share" of their economy, the main difference being the *German* firms are primarily family owned with a long-term perspective, while in the U.S. most are publically traded, short-term profits driven.

We used to be *Germany* at least in terms of being the most successful advanced economy. There might be some lessons to be learned or re-learned here.

[58]

Think Small

Our Government is accustomed to thinking big. Too big. Big plans, big programs, big bailouts, big corporations, big taxes, big deficits, big agencies, world domination, big armies, big salaries, big campaign donors, etc. They should try thinking small, particularly when it comes to business. Every mega corporation was once a small business. Every business starts small. I've been a small business owner and I know how tough it is. Not only do you have to raise capital, deal with competition and a have a challenge attracting customers you've got the government constantly in your pockets extracting their tribute. Business licenses, fees, permits, quarterly tax reports, sales tax collections and payments, inspections, etc.

The government needs to change its approach from control, regulating, and taxing, to one of facilitating, enabling, promoting and nurturing small enterprises and entrepreneurs across this nation. These nascent companies are our economic future. Government priorities are all screwed up. They bailout and grant favors to the giants while squashing the infants. This isn't a long-range plan. Invest in the future, or at least don't raise the hurdles so high that only a few can complete the race. Already 9 out of 10 new businesses don't survive the first five years. It sometimes appears as though the government is aiming for 10 of 10.

What the Debt Means to You

It might help to personalize debt. When we read "National Debt" it's easy to think of it as the country owing money, but the country is comprised of individuals and we each share in the obligation. Your share is over $53,000 (per *Senate Budget Committee*). I hope we're not asked to pay up anytime soon! And just to put this amount in perspective we can compare it with other nations. It's larger than *Greece* ($39,384), *Italy* ($41,645), *France* ($37,104), *Spain* ($27,637) or *Portugal* ($23,857).

[59]

Perhaps you've seen the acronym *PIGS*. Economists used this short-hand when referring to the Southern European countries of *Portugal*, *Italy*, *Greece* and *Spain*. Those countries are poster-kids for troubled economies in the *European Union*. This is not good company to be in. Of course politicians and many economists will say we're different. We are much larger economy, we hold Reserve Currency status, our economy is more capable of improvement, we don't have as many so-cialized aspects, etc. Rubbish. Nations are either fiscally responsible or not. And we're not.

Does Free Enterprise Still Work?

This country thrived in a free enterprise system, although globaliza-tion, de-industrialization, regulation, automation, international competition, have all played a role in our decline. Many, including this author, would argue the government's over-regulation has been a detriment to sustained economic growth. Certainly our government's economic policies have "stimulated" the rich, devastated the middle class, and engorged the numbers of poor. A bag of tricks that will cer-tainly backfire; it's just a matter of time till this nasty "pain game" ends. Our economic system requires resuscitation— it's an emergen-cy. Either the government must get out of the way of private enterprise or take a more supportive role.

Chapter Six

The Election Trick

The election trick is a very sneaky one and involves everything from depriving you of your right to vote, gerrymandering election districts, creating physical, documentation or procedural barriers at the polling place, improper ordering of candidates on the ballot, limitation of "qualified" candidates and parties, coercing you to follow "party lines", etc. Other tricks include convincing you a candidate's platform is something they really plan to achieve, as well as deceptive reporting and forecasting of election results.

.

Someone asked me: Why do we keep electing these fools to office? Why can't we make better choices? Well, there's an easy answer, WE DON'T HAVE MUCH TO CHOOSE FROM. Nobody in their right mind would want to be President, on the chance that they will be in the history books, have a Library, or even grace a coin or currency with their likeness. You'd almost have to be a real patriot, and God knows there aren't many of them around anymore. But you could be power-hungry, greedy or have an Ego the size of *Texas*. Or, more likely you could be a part of a political machine, one designed to propel you into, arguably, the most powerful office on the planet.

Lots of Parties

There are over twenty parties with candidates eligible for the Presidential ballot. Some of these you're familiar with such as the: *Libertarian Party, Green Party, Peace and Freedom Party, and perhaps the Justice Party.*

But there's also the American's Elect Party, Party for Socialism and Liberation, Independent Party, Socialist Party, Socialist Workers Party, etc. I won't list them all, particularly the ones that gained no ballot access like the *Boston Tea Party* or the *Whig Party*.

So why did I say "we don't have much to choose from?" Because we don't, and because many of these candidates are either "vanity" candidates who want to say they ran for president, or they have a nominal chance, or not a prayer of winning. Most people wouldn't consider voting for the smallest party's candidates as they believe it's "throwing your vote away."

The presidential election campaigns have become media contests focusing on who will have the cleverest commercial, make a mistake, or unintentionally speak the truth. The debates are "Beauty Contests" like the *Miss America* pageant, *American Idol*, or *Dancing with the Stars*. Important things like Character, Ability or Track Record don't count for much. Who looks the most appealing; who can deliver the glibbest "sound bites;" or dance around the issues, who can speak most convincingly while saying nothing of significance?

Political Campaigns are Expensive

The campaigns are high stakes theatre and at the presidential and congressional levels are funded by hundreds of millions, even hundreds of billions of dollars.

"The best government money can buy" is an often-heard refrain. But of course money can't buy the best government. It's probably just the opposite.

When a candidate or office-holder owes his position to big donors and special interests how concerned can they be with us?

Impact of Advertising on Elections

Elections have become obscenely expensive, and most of that money is spent on Campaign advertising. More than three million ads costing $2 billion were aired during the 2012 election. They're not spending that money for nothing. In a sense they're trying to "buy" the election.

Think of campaigns in terms of "selling" the candidate, not unlike the marketing campaigns that are designed to get you to purchase products like mouthwash or toilet paper.

The message is "higher quality," "longer lasting," "more colorful," "superior," "more durable," and more consistent with your lifestyle.

However, in recent years most of these ads are negative and appeal to anger, bias, frustration, fear or other such emotions. These ads don't focus so much on the qualities of your candidate (product) rather they emphasize the negative qualities of the competition. Think: Crummy product, lower quality, less colorful, inferior, less durable and inconsistent with your lifestyle. Worse than the ads infer: dangerous, unacceptable perhaps disastrous results if you "buy" the *other* product (candidate).

According to experts, in the 2012 election 70% of the advertising fell into the negative category (compared with 9% in 2008!). Fully 60% of these ads were sponsored by outside groups (rather than the Party or Candidate). You probably don't recognize many of the sponsors as they are primarily "fronts" for the political parties.

Here are the big spenders during the 2012 General Election: *Crossroads, Americans for Prosperity, American Energy Alliance, American Future Fund, Priorities USA Action, Environmental Defense, American Petroleum Institute, AFSCME, American Crossroads.* One of the first observations you may have is how positive and patriotic most of these organizations sound. The names often include "American" and positive terms like "prosperity," and "future." Yet these organizations are sponsoring such negative ads. Interesting.

Leave Your Brain at Home

When you go to your polling place to vote, the mainstream candidates hope you'll leave your brain at home, and so do their supporters.

Several of the minor parties may appeal to your intellect as they have a more well-defined, perhaps controversial, platform that they want you to consider.

And they'll want to demonstrate the contrast between themselves and the big D & R candidates. But the big two are hoping you won't look too hard or deep. After all, they and their supporters have spent a ~~small~~ large fortune to get elected by appealing to your baser emotions.

And those supporters hope to gain something in return.

Try to set your emotions aside. During an election the country's future depends on your thoughtful consideration of the issues and your analysis of each candidate's potential for leadership (as outlined in Chapter 22).

Remember, they're "Out to Get You" -- YOUR VOTE!

Campaign Financing Reform

Campaign financing reform should be a top priority, only then would we see the best candidates and have the opportunity to vote for them. Perhaps then we would discover some real "gems" among candidates vying for the highest office. They might even emerge from the marginal parties where many idealists seem to reside.

Everyone should be on an equal financial footing when it comes to holding office. The richest candidates or those who are in the pockets of the wealthiest individuals and corporations cannot be fair, even-handed, and objective in their governance, even if they want to. However, as a result of a 2010 ruling the limitations on contributions from corporations and organizations are for all practical purposes non-existent. And, again citing First Amendment free speech principles, in October, 2013 the *Supreme Court* may further weaken campaign finance laws by striking down the $123,200 every two years limit making it even easier for individual to buy their piece of the Government.

At every level of government having qualified, principled candidates to choose from is a problem. Typically, the most qualified people do not want the job, and those who can easily be corrupted do.

Why Become a Politician?

It seems you get to choose from four types: 1) Individuals who want the power, prestige or connections of public office, 2) those who want to "give back to their communities," and/or 3) the independently wealthy who may also want to do one of the aforementioned, and, most common of all, 4) the tool of the power brokers. Of course a candidate can have multiple characteristics and categories. Whatever category the candidate falls into, he or she will have to have a substantial amount of money, be good at raising it, and/or have deep-pocketed sponsors.

An example of a politician who exemplifies the first three types combined is *Michael Bloomberg*, former Mayor of *New York City*. He seems to enjoy the spotlight, wants to give back to the community, is independently wealthy, and exercised the power and prestige of the office. But did he go too far? He appeared to have an additional personal agenda in that he thought he knew what's best for *New Yorkers*. He didn't think big sodas are good for the public, or excessive idling of vehicles, or trans-fats.

A state court overturned his restriction on sodas over 15oz, saying that he exceeded his mayoral authority. He appealed the decision, but the Appeals Court upheld the ruling. Talk about overreach!

Note to elected officials: Imposing your personal view on your constituency is not a good idea. You're not royalty and they're not your subjects! The good mayor and many other public officials are only too happy telling us what we should and should not do.

Fair Elections?

Elections are not fair in this country. There's no level playing field and we don't have the best candidates. Candidates with the most money generally win, and once in office incumbents are almost always reelected.

Name recognition is an important factor although campaign cash is "King." Reelection rates for the Senate are over 80% and in the House of Representatives average an incredible 90%!

America has never had "clean" elections. Politics is a dirty business and with so much money and power at stake shenanigans are pulled every election at every level. Some of the tricks include: "Stuffing" ballot boxes, limitations on voter eligibility, inconvenient location of polling places, names missing from registered voter lists, gerrymandering of districts to gain advantage, restrictions on early voting, shorter hours at polling places, electronic manipulation of data, missing ballots, improperly counted ballots, leaving candidates' names off ballots, casting fraudulent absentee ballots, requiring "picture" I.D.'s, etc. Perhaps the most mysterious and infamous election was the 2000 Presidential Election. It was a close election and on election night the contest came down to one deciding State - *Florida*. And the election remained undecided with no clear victor for several days. *Al Gore* the *Democrat* and *George W. Bush* the *Republican* candidate were "neck and neck" with only a few votes separating them. The winner would gain *Florida*'s Electoral College votes and be elected President!

Fortunately for Mr. Bush, the deciding State was *Florida* where his brother *Jeb Bush* was Governor, and *Katherine Harris*, *Florida*'s Secretary of State happened to be his election campaign co-chair. To help matters even more, seven of the nine *Supreme Court* Justices were appointed by *Republican* Presidents, four of those by his father (*George H.W. Bush*). If you think in this situation *Al Gore* had the slightest chance of winning, you aren't thinking straight.

[67]

During the election *Florida* had developed several strategies to neutralize the Black vote. First was a "felons list." Because statistically Blacks were over-represented, with higher percentages of convicted convicts and under *Florida* law, felons weren't allowed to vote. Second, ballots were scanned for "validity" and interestingly, ballots cast by African-Americans were ruled invalid at a rate 10x that of White or Hispanic voters.

I'm sure some of you may remember the "hanging chads" and the scenes of election officials holding each up to a light to see if pieces of paper were "hanging" from the punched cards which *Florida* used at that time (supposed evidence of a mistake). It finally boiled down to the uncounted Absentee Ballots. When these ballots were reviewed; in pro-*Bush* Counties 530 were accepted and counted, while 523 were rejected; in pro-*Gore* Counties 150 were accepted and counted but 666 were declared invalid. This disparity sealed the election.

After all was said and done *Bush* won *Florida* by a mere 533 votes and the Supreme Court validated his election as President. The rest is history. *Al Gore* became a political has-been, and climate change alarmist, while *President Bush* went on to lead the country into war, confusion and despair.

Gerrymandering is a BIG Problem

Although I've briefly touched on the issue of gerrymandering and stated that a major election problem is "not much to choose from" this area deserves more explanation. Gerrymandering is the process of defining electoral district boundaries by using a methodology which gains unfair advantage for particular parties or politicians. Essentially, demographics are analyzed and in most scenarios likely favorable voters are aggregated into a defined geographic area.

The term (according to *Merriam-Webster*) dates to 1812 when, under *Elbridge Gerry*'s Governorship in *Massachusetts*, a district was formed which resembled a salamander. The combination of his last name (*Gerry*) and a portion of the word sala*mander* were used to form the term.

You might think that voting districts are in a grid of neatly defined squares or rectangles drawn fairly within state and county boundaries. Not so.

Your tricky politicians want to keep getting re-elected so the parties design districts filled with likely voters *for them*. The system results in entrenched politicians in largely non-competitive districts.

For example, consider this: Your elected official knows that his or her voters are generally White, middle-class, and conservative, so logically he would seek to run for office in a district with a preponderance of these types of individuals. So they work with state and local officials to create and maintain districts to make that happen.

According to data provided in a 2012 *Princeton* (*Wang, Sam*) study, *Republicans* are "better" at using this technique than *Democrats* and the States with the most "offenses" are: *Pennsylvania*, *Texas*, *Ohio*, *North Carolina*, *Michigan*, *Arizona*, *Virginia*, *Illinois*, and *Indiana*.

The result is less competitive, strange-looking districts which are by design more homogeneous. Theoretically you might have a district one block wide and five miles long! It also results in a polarization of political views and candidates making it difficult to achieve compromise in legislative bodies. The practice is widespread and contributes to political dysfunctionality. Corrupt, sure. Practical, yes.

Election Hypocrites and a Vindication

It's always intriguing to me how we are constantly critical of, and offer to monitor the fairness of, elections in other Countries while we seemingly ignore major manipulation of our own election results.

According to *Range Voting Org.* many U.S. Presidents owe elections, at some point in their career, to corruption and fraud. Among them: *Harry S. Truman, John F. Kennedy, Lyndon B. Johnson, Richard M. Nixon,* and as detailed in the preceding, *George W. Bush.*

Incidentally, the only U.S. President who had a meaningful role in U.S. election reform was *Jimmy Carter.* Not my favorite President but an honest man.

When running for the State Senate in *Georgia* Mr. *Carter* was cheated out of his win by a crooked political boss *Joe Hurst.* He went on to sue and the ensuing court investigation "discovered" enough "missing" ballots to reverse the election results and *Carter* was finally declared the winner.

Chapter Seven

The Welfare Trick

A simple trick based on a profound premise: The more people can be made to be dependent, the more passive they become and the less inclined to challenge the status quo. If the government is the sponsor of dependency, and the electorate has an increasing percentage of dependent individuals, the more likely they are to vote for those who will perpetuate these programs.

During the 2012 Presidential election campaign *Mitt Romney*, the *Republican* candidate, at a fundraising event, famously said: "There are 47% of the people who will vote for the president [*Barack Obama*] no matter what." He went on to say: These are the people..."who are dependent on government, who believe that they are victims, that the government has responsibility to care for them, who believe that they're entitled to healthcare, to food, to housing, to you name it." This offhanded and ill-advised remark may have cost *Romney* the election. Especially when someone at the event videotaped him and it ended up spread it all over the internet and the media. Romney seemed callous and uncaring; a rich man with no empathy for the poor.

He was correct, of course, at least in a statistical sense. In fact, according to the *Washington Post* he understated the true prevalence of government aid—it was really higher than that– 49%! It's probably over 50% by now! Of course, as with everything there's more than just numbers here.

The vast majority of government program beneficiaries are the elderly, and the biggest program is *Social Security*. *Social Security* is not welfare, and many seniors resented the callous *Romney* characterization of them as "dependent" and "victims." It's a program the preponderance of recipients has contributed to throughout their working lives. *Romney*, like every good politician obviously knew how to mislead with statistical data. But it backfired on him. And, to imply that *Republicans* don't receive government benefits really took the prize!

Unintended Consequences

I have some personal history with welfare programs. In the mid-1960's I was a Social Worker in South-Central *Los Angeles*. (Roughly *Compton*, *Watts* and *Exposition Park* vicinity.) A hard-core poverty area. I saw first-hand what the *Kennedy* and *Johnson* administrations' initiatives did to families. While I'm certain these were well-intentioned programs, the *"New Frontier"* and the *"Great Society"* spawned unanticipated, highly negative social consequences. In essence, the *AFDC* (Aid to Families with Dependent Children) program disproportionately impacted minorities (because more of them were in the poorer income categories). The *AFDC* program had a central feature that was anti-family. "Deprivation" it was termed. Eligibility required it. The legal definition, codified into welfare eligibility rules, meant that children had to be deprived of the care and support of one of their parents. So, millions of family units were disrupted or destroyed as the programs gained acceptance and momentum. Think of it in this way: Your government went into competition with the male heads of households of poor families. As rational human beings, poor women throughout the nation did some quick financial calculations. Were they better off with him (the father of their child) or without him?

If they got rid of him the U.S. government would provide the mother with a monthly stipend for each of her children until the child(ren) turned 18. Tempting, huh? A steady, predictable income with which to meet life's necessities—something many of these women and their families had never experienced before.

This began an explosion of single parent households. A neat trick! And a socially destructive one. American society was changed forever. Young males with no father figure. Young females with a government dependent mother as a role model. And, while I wouldn't be so callous, or naïve to say that many families were not helped, on the balance I believe it was an overall negative. And of course many amazing, talented and successful people have emerged from the ranks of the welfare dependent families. However, other solutions like ones providing temporary subsistence while emphasizing employment and job training for husbands and unmarried fathers would have been preferable from a social standpoint, in my opinion.

And programs such as *Food Stamps (SNAP- Supplemental Nutrition Assistance Program)* and other means-tested cash, food, and housing programs also foster dependency. Sure people need help and, as we discovered earlier in this book *most of us will at some point,* but it's a seductive trap.

Just as the government seduced poor mothers into abandoning the father of their children, the government has increased their outreach to seduce many others into abandoning their jobs, dreams and independence. Instead of limiting their efforts to competing with minority fathers, the government now competes with the entire private sector and our capitalistic system.

Government assistance programs are never "free," they always come with a hidden cost, and programs like *AFDC (now TANF – Temporary Financial Assistance to Needy Families), Food Stamps (now SNAP Supplemental Nutrition Assistance Program), Section 8 Housing,* free lifeline cell-phones, *UIB,* disability benefits, are only the tip of the iceberg. The *USA.gov* website describes the whole array of benefits. These programs provide only enough to survive, never enough to progress. The fortunate recipients recognize this and want more.

An example of another well-intentioned program gone awry, the *Federal Disability Insurance* Program has grown exponentially and is rife with fraud. A *60 Minutes* special (*Disability USA*) aired on October 6, 2013 investigated the allegations. According to disability judge, *Marilyn Zahm*: "If the American public knew what was going on in our system, half would be outraged and the other half would apply for benefits." Senator Tom Coburn of Oklahoma claims that half the recipients "don't deserve it."

Government assistance programs were initiated to help recipients regain independence. But everyone can't, and unfortunately some won't. The gamesmanship occurs on both sides. The Government creates demand by offering an ever-expanding array of services.

The parasitic members of society quickly recognize the opportunities for enrichment and avail themselves of undeserved benefits, thereby exhausting resources, driving up costs and depriving those genuinely in need from securing necessary help.

In addition, many benefit recipients become so comfortable or disillusioned that they drop out of productive society. The deck is stacked against them anyway, so it may be a rational decision, or not even a decision at all but the course of least resistance. I don't blame them. I fault the system.

When even one American - who has done nothing wrong - is forced by fear to shut his mind and close his mouth - then all Americans are in peril.

--Harry S. Truman

If you can't convince them, confuse them.

--Harry S. Truman

Those who want the Government to regulate matters of the mind and spirit are like men who are so afraid of being murdered that they commit suicide to avoid assassination.

Harry S. Truman

Chapter Eight

The Healthcare Trick

The healthcare trick can cost you your health or your life. Even if it doesn't, it may bankrupt you. The government is one of the biggest healthcare sponsors and providers in the country and they want to get bigger. The trick is to get you to believe they can make it better and more cost-effective when we all know the government to be inefficient and wasteful.

It's true we have the "best healthcare in the world," but it's the most costly too. In addition there is a byzantine complexity, and many barriers to obtaining this "world class" healthcare. Insurance, pre-existing conditions, limited coverage, pre-authorization, are just a few of the many hurdles and limitations. If you're wealthy or have excellent insurance coverage, or are a member of Congress it's great. If not, navigating the healthcare system will be more of a challenge.

Many people are dependent on the government for the cost of their healthcare, and even if they're not they are still involved in a system which is heavily regulated by government agencies. The government's oversight is arguably necessary to insure quality of care, although as in the education system there are numerous professional associations, boards, and public and private accrediting and watchdog agencies involved. But the extent of government involvement has complicated the system and increased overall costs. Restrictions and cutbacks on levels of governmental reimbursement have also turned healthcare providers into liars.

In order to obtain sufficient reimbursement in face of these restrictions the classification of treatments and procedures (medical records coding) has become a questionable art-form. Combined with insanely inflated costs for technology, pharmaceuticals and malpractice insurance obtaining and paying for healthcare has become a major headache and huge cost for most Americans.

The Healthcare Monster

To *President Obama*'s credit, he tackled the issue just as the *Clinton* administration had before him. But unlike *Hillary Clinton* he got much further. The *Obama* administration's *Affordable Healthcare* program was converted into an Act passed by Congress. Then, as it became more real, opposition swelled from all corners. Business owners said the cost of insuring their employees would drive them out of business, healthcare providers indicated it might drive them out of business as well.

Congress found the costs too high, providers thought the reimbursement too low. The signature, some would say singular, accomplishment of his administration, and consequently his legacy was in trouble.

"*Obamacare*" as it's known by critics and supporters alike, was intended to achieve "universal healthcare" at lower cost. It was literally rammed through Congress in the middle of the night on Christmas Eve. Interestingly, the Xmas eve vote was the first time this had happened since the Senate had an emergency vote concerning the military in 1895; it was the infamous bill that Senators didn't have a chance to read before voting on it. The program is partially funded through massive multi-billion dollar budgetary transfers from *Medicare,* and eventually, perhaps through co-pays, and employer employee insurance fees.

The *CBO* (Congressional Budget Office) admits that universal healthcare will not be achieved through this plan. By their calculations thirty million people will remain uncovered *ten years* after implementation. And sadly, another 12-20 million workers already covered may lose their existing employer sponsored health care coverage.

There is a cynical provision that assesses a $2,000 penalty for employers who do not comply, but this is much less than the annual insurance premium for the typical employee and their family. Then, if they lose their employee sponsored healthcare, these uncovered employees can participate in the state-sponsored and tax-subsidized exchange program(s). This results in shifting costs from businesses to taxpayers.

And because the law applies to businesses with more than fifty employees, companies with less than that are freezing hiring and those with more are laying off employees or using part-time workers. What a mess!

The incredibly high costs for consumer health insurance, medical education, pharmaceuticals, medical equipment, malpractice insurance, office and hospital space, nursing, supportive and ancillary services, laboratory, etc. all drive up the cost of healthcare, but so do Government requirements and restrictions. "*Obamacare*" the *Affordable Healthcare Act* was intended to address the high cost to consumers through a plethora of requirements, primarily related to coverage and insurance. As V.P. *Joe Biden* articulately said: "it's a big fuck**g deal!" The *AMA* (American Medical Association) endorses the plan with some reservations. Individual physicians support enhanced coverage and improved access but remain skeptical about "red tape" and reimbursement changes.

However, Congress is shielded from the effects of *Obamacare*. Members of Congress were not actually exempted from the law but, according to a August 5, 2013 *Wall Street Journal* article, through a sneaky back-door arrangement between the White House and the *OMB* they were granted additional pay so that they will not experience any coverage or compensation loss. Will the trickery ever end? I think you know the answer.

This byzantine law involves fees, penalties, new federal agencies and expansion of existing departments, etc. The bill (HR 3962) is 1990 pages in length and contains 363,086 words. Full implementation is scheduled to take several years (until 2018) with provisions, requirements and mandates for individuals, employers, physicians, insurance and healthcare providers, etc. There are review boards, patient counseling requirements and changes in physician service delivery and reimbursement provisions. Coverage exemptions have already been provided to several politically connected unions, some local governments and school districts, and scores of companies. Once they find out all the costs, I'm sure there will be more added to the growing list.

Marketing of Obamacare

As mentioned in Chapter Five, I was just finishing up this book at the beginning of October, 2013, the rollout of *Obamacare* and the Congressional approval of the fiscal year budget along with an increase in the Debt limit were all colliding. Name-calling was in full force with *Tea Party Republicans* leading the charge to defund the *Affordable Healthcare Act*. The marketing of *Obamacare* had, at that point, been going on for years.

The legislation was off to a rocky start following the classic and questionable last minute ramming of the legislation through the Senate on Christmas Eve in 2009, and the quotable comment by H.R. Speaker, *Nancy Pelosi* asking members to "pass the bill so you can find out what's in it, away from the fog of controversy."

Vote for it now, you can read it later, it was the message. Disturbing at a minimum in a democracy where the people's interests require thoughtful, considered review and deliberation of *any* proposal prior to adoption. Particularly one as important to the public and massive in scale as this one. But this was purely political. And there were a bundle of textbook examples of political trickery and manipulation to follow.

Now it was almost four years later with *Affordable Healthcare* State Insurance Exchange signups scheduled to begin in a few days, and the legislation was still in upheaval. *President Obama* and his minions were busy touting the benefits and accusing the *Republicans* of threatening a shutdown of the Government for political reasons. The *Republicans* responded by carving out *Obamacare* for defunding while funding all other programs and services. Political drama once again.

President Obama's marketing effort included a widely covered promotional meeting with well-liked former *President Clinton* and spouse and presidential aspirant *Hillary Rodham Clinton* at the *Clinton Foundation* Center.

The following day newspaper headlines across the country announced "U.S.: Obamacare Cost Below Forecast." And these huge government programs always begin this way. Low cost, great coverage.

As *Ronald Reagan* once said: "The nine most terrifying words in the English language are: "I'm from the government and I'm here to help."

Government programs are sold on the basis of service, necessity, or benefit. The advocates stress the benefits and minimize the costs. They seldom turn out as expected. Just like Flood Insurance or Windstorm (hurricane) Insurance, Affordable Housing, etc. they quickly morph into high cost, mandatory government-sponsored entities. It's like a "bait and switch" con. Sucker people in, gain their support, then rob them blind. The Health Exchange private insurers must be barely able to contain their glee at this opportunity.

Medicare Fraud

Doing business with the Government can be quite profitable and attractive to ethically compromised entrepreneurs. As a consequence there are plenty of crooks in the business.

I currently live in *Miami*. This city is very entrepreneurial and hundreds of health care related businesses have sprung up. Unfortunately this area is also considered the *Medicare/Medicaid* fraud capitol of the country. Not a pleasant distinction but a very real one. In this town, perhaps in yours too, it seems the government is always trying to close one provider or supplier or another. Here in *Miami* they've found a fertile hunting ground, in a nice tropical climate, for their investigators and auditors. Here are some examples.

[82]

Excerpt from: **Department of Justice**
Office of Public Affairs bulletin
May 14, 2013

In Miami, a total of 25 defendants, including two nurses, a para-medic and a radiographer, were charged today and yesterday for their participation in various fraud schemes involving a total of $44 million in false billings for home health care, mental health services, occupational and physical therapy, DME and HIV infusion. In one case, three defendants were charged for participating in a $20 million home health fraud scheme involving a home health agency, Trust Care Health Services. Court documents allege that the defendants bribed Medicare beneficiaries for their Medicare information, which was used to bill for home health services that were not rendered or that were not medically necessary. According to court documents, the lead defendant spent much of the money from the scheme, and purchased multiple luxury vehicles, including two Lamborghinis, a Ferrari and a Bentley.

A psychiatrist who has been practicing in Miami since the 1970s was arrested Tuesday along with six therapists on charges of scheming to steal $63 million from the taxpayer-funded Medicare program.
Roger Rousseau, 71, the former medical director for a defunct mental-health clinic operation, was indicted on charges of conspiring to commit health care fraud. Rousseau, who had his first appearance along with the other defendants in federal court, was released on a $375,000 bond. —*Miami Herald* (7/17/2013)

The preceding examples are a tiny tip of a humongous iceberg of corruption and fraud. The primary methods are: Phantom Billing, Patient Kickbacks, and Upcoding Procedures. The phantom billing scheme involves billing the government for procedures not performed. Patient kickbacks involve obtaining valid *Medicare* numbers from eligible beneficiaries by paying a bribe for them.

[83]

Upcoding means identifying more expensive procedures (than the ones received) for inflated reimbursement purposes. An attractive feature of the *Affordable Healthcare Act* increases funding for detecting and prosecuting *Medicare* fraud. I applaud this provision.

Now here's an interesting tidbit. One of the biggest examples of fraud in the history of *Medicare* was investigated at *Columbia/HCA*, the largest private for-profit healthcare company in the U.S. The corporation utilized each of the dishonest methods described in the previous paragraphs. In 2001 the corporation pled guilty to more than a dozen criminal and civil charges but negotiated a settlement with the U.S. Government. Total costs of the civil settlements were over $1.7 billion, in addition to numerous government fines and paybacks to State and Federal *Medicare* and *Medicaid* agencies. The corporation changed its name back to *HCA* (*Hospital Corporation of America*) and is still in business. The CEO (*Rick Scott*) was fired without facing criminal charges and was *elected Governor of Florida in 2010.*

I suspect that you're beginning to realize that healthcare is rife with fraud and that the government tacitly condones it. Perhaps it's because the industry spends so much supporting politicians.

International Comparison of Healthcare

An international comparison reveals some interesting similarities and differences. The *World Health Organization* (*WHO*) looked at health care delivery systems in 6 highly developed countries.

As we all suspected the U.S. is the most costly. But cost alone is not the most meaningful comparison.

The analysis is quite detailed and I will not reproduce all of the charts and data for you, (but if you're interested you can find the report at www.who.int/bulletin/archieves/78(6)770). Another, more recent analysis came from *PBS.*

The most recent data has been used in all cases, as the main discrepancies resulted from the differences in timeframes and the fact that the reference countries were not identical. For instance, whereas *WHO* compared the U.S. with the *U.K., Germany, France, Denmark and Sweden*; *PBS* used *OCED* (Organization for Economic Cooperation and Development) data which includes thirty-four countries. Obviously, the most meaningful comparisons for us are those with the richest, most highly developed members of that broader group. The conclusions from both organizations are remarkably similar, however.

Healthcare in the U.S. absorbs 17.6% of *GDP* significantly more than the next highest, the *Netherlands* at 12%. For comparison it is only 9.6% in the U.K. and 11.6% in *Germany*. *France, Canada* and *Switzerland* are also in the 11% range. *Britain* definitely has a low cost system among our peers.

Annual expenditures per capita range from a high of $8,233 in the U.S. to a low of $913 in *Turkey*. *Germany* is $4,338 and *Norway* is $5,388. The average for all 34 *OCED* countries is $3,268. The U.S. is about two and one-half times higher than that.

Drug expenditures are lower in *Denmark* and highest in the U.S., with *Germany* and *France* coming in next. When it comes to *MRI*'s they're not quite on every corner but the U.S. has twice as many to five times as many as comparable countries. Costly equipment and a costly procedure. The same with *CT Scanners* - again we're the high end outlier. But when it comes to hospital beds per capita we're the lowest! *France* and *Germany* have twice as many; we're even lower than the *United Kingdom*.

In terms of Physicians and Nurses per capita we're roughly comparable to the others, except for the *U.K.* which is quite low in number of nurses.

Significantly higher wages for health care professionals and administration along with much higher accessibility of medical technology in America appear to explain the substantial difference in cost between the U.S. and the other highly developed nations studied.

For example administrative costs in the U.S. total $900 per person, almost as much as the total annual healthcare cost per capita in *Turkey* and three times the administrative component ($300) in *France*.

U.S. frequency and cost for certain conditions is also considerably higher. For example, a coronary bypass operation costs 50% more in this country than it would in *Canada*, *Australia* or *France*. Likewise with hip and knee replacements. We also have much higher rates of tonsillectomies and Caesarean sections. And high rates of *MRI*'s, and asthma treatments.

Where the U.S. performs well is in lower numbers of physicians, lower wait times, vastly more research, a shorter drug approval process, innovative treatments, safer hospitals, higher quality of care, shorter hospital stays, fewer physician consultations and better outcomes particularly with cancer.

Despite having the world's best and safest healthcare system Americans don't live as long as people do in many other countries. 78.7 years is the average lifespan in America, that's lower than the 79.8 years for the average of all *OCED* nations. It appears as though the main reason for this is an "epidemic" of obesity. The only nation with a higher percentage of fat people amongst the 34 countries studied was *Greece*.

The *WHO* report indicates a narrowing of the cost differential over the past decade This suggests that greater efficiency and cost-containment is occurring organically.

Will "Affordable Healthcare" Help?

Does *Obamacare* address the major issues identified in this chapter? Yes, partially it does. But the *Affordable Health Care Act* focuses primarily on the marketplace purchase of insurance coverage and not on other major sources of the problem. There is, however, a provision to dramatically increase the Government's investigatory scope and to step up enforcement and prosecution to root out entrenched and oppor-tunistic fraud. This is an important positive initiative.

Other positive features include: Elimination of lifetime caps on healthcare insurer payouts, no denial of coverage for pre-existing con-ditions, and children can remain on their parents' health plan until age twenty-six. But these positive elements come at a cost and the disrup-tion in the healthcare industry cannot be foreseen.

Left unfettered the marketplace will eventually determine the cost of everything. The government has power, through sheer size and regu-latory provisions to influence behavior. The loose reimbursement control system for *Medicare* spawned a cottage industry of shady en-trepreneurs to exploit its vulnerabilities contributing to the high cost of medical care. The government's (over) protection of the pharmaceuti-cal industry drives drug costs up. Whenever they disturb the dynamics of the marketplace there will be unintended consequences and I fear that their increased involvement in the healthcare industry will not have the desired effect.

The viability and impact of *Obamacare* is yet to be determined. All large government programs have had their supporters and detractors. All have had mixed results and unanticipated consequences. *Obama-care* joins the ranks of programs like *Social Security, Medicare, Public Assistance (Welfare) programs, Food Stamps, Housing Assistance*, etc. We'll see.

Every government degenerates
when trusted to the rulers of the people alone.
The people themselves are its only safe depositories.

Thomas Jefferson

I am neither bitter nor cynical but I do wish
there was less immaturity in political thinking.

--Franklin D. Roosevelt

The government, which was designed for the people,
has got into the hands of the bosses
and their employers, the special interests.
An invisible empire has been set up above the forms of
democracy.

--Woodrow Wilson

Chapter Nine

The Crime Trick

The crime trick is insidious and harmful to society. The trick is to get us to believe the most dangerous criminals are drug users, whistle-blowers, petty criminals, welfare cheats, and the like, while corporations, politicians, wall-street bankers, etc. steal with impunity. Another part is to make you feel insecure and fearful and look to the government to protect and rescue you.

You probably know that we have more people in prison than any other country in the world. More than *Russia*, more than *China*, more than totalitarian regimes or dictatorships. Are we Americans that bad? The worst people on the planet? Probably not!

There are a couple of reasons for this costly, socially destructive rate of incarceration. First, the legal profession is big business in this nation - so is the criminal justice system. Crime is big business at all levels of government with scores of agencies and departments involved.

"War" on Drugs?

But the biggest reasons can probably be traced to the "War on Drugs," the unwinnable war that's been going on for years, and Mandatory Minimum Sentences which lock up offenders for lengthy periods, sometimes for life, and often for minor, non-violent offenses. In fact, some years ago, a friend of mine was faced with a 30/life sentence under *California*'s "Three Strikes" law. The poor man was an addict. It did neither him nor society any good to lock him up for a lifetime. Fortunately, with character witnesses, and a good attorney a sympathetic judge recognized the folly of the situation, "struck" (erased/removed) one of his prior strikes so that he was not faced with the third strike and a wasted life. Instead he served a shorter sentence and was diverted to a drug rehabilitation program.

At a news conference on August 12, 2013 U.S. Attorney General *Eric Holder,* who had an unimpressive record, announced a major policy recommendation to be implemented by federal prosecutors. Under his proposal low-level, non-violent offenders would not be subjected to mandatory minimum jail/prison sentences. Whatever your politics this represents a major step forward, providing Congress concurs.

Our government's history of involvement with the drug cartel is particularly disturbing. From the *CIA* importation, in the 1970's and 1980's, of illegal drugs ostensibly supplied by *Panamanian* leader *Noriega*, to involvement with the *Mexican* cartel in more recent years. And the *ATF* (Alcohol, Tobacco, and Firearms) agency supplying weapons to gun runners who supplied weapons to the *Mexican* cartels in 2010.

True to form the federal agencies facilitating the *"Fast and Furious"* Operation lost track of hundreds of the weapons, one of which, ironically, ended up killing another government employee, a *Border Patrol* agent.

It's a very strange scenario with federal agencies facilitating the importation of drugs destined for users and addicts in this country, and supplying weapons to the cartel while coincidentally arresting hapless customers for violations of domestic drug laws. Is this insanity, or what?

It certainly fuels a large, counter-productive interrelated government system where we help cartels, in hopes of entrapping them, while increasing drug flow into the country, ensnaring more susceptible citizens into drug dependence, then incentivizing police to arrest these people, and finally incarcerating them in jails or prisons at public expense. A not-so-clever trick with disastrous consequences!

I recently viewed an interesting film titled *"How to Make Money Selling Drugs."* Naturally, the film, although it had won critical acclaim, was not in wide release. I saw it at a small Art Cinema in *Miami*. The movie made an impact. A documentary, it featured public officials, drug dealers, drug users and drug "Lords," politicians, celebrities, *FBI* and *CIA* operatives, police and prison officials. The point was: The legal and enforcement processes have created a national "monster." Police Departments all over the nation would prefer to chase drug dealers, growers and transporters rather than solve other types of crimes because of the financial incentives associated with "drug busts." The "asset forfeiture" laws often require minimal proof in order to seize money or property. With tight budgets in municipalities and states, even at the federal level, it's extremely tempting to devote disproportionate resources to drug crimes in expectation of sharing in the "proceeds" from the bust. Then staff can be expanded and new law enforcement equipment purchased. All law enforcement agencies can participate. It's a multi-billion dollar business.

Billions for law enforcement, hundreds of millions for the drug deal-ers, hundreds of millions for the over-worked court system, and billions for the penal system. Isn't it time we re-examined this? And recently some States (*Washington* and *Colorado*) have, decriminaliz-ing small quantities of marijuana for personal use. A recent investigation of a claim made at the *Brickyard 400* NASCAR race in July, 2013 on a giant screen at that event was fact-checked by *Politi-Fact*. The message implied marijuana is less harmful than alcohol and included the headline: "A New Beer?" The fact checking included research of medical data concerning the "toxicity" of each substance. The conclusion: "Mostly True." Marijuana is less harmful and signif-icantly less toxic.

Personally, I'm not a drug advocate or a drug user. I know that with my personality I had better stay away. I might like the feeling. And, I probably wouldn't be able to control it. I don't believe I would enjoy the consequences of over-indulgence in hard drugs such as living un-der a bridge, going to jail or panhandling.

Punishment or Rehabilitation

Its not completely unfair to consider our Criminal Justice system a failure. The front end, the police and the courts, serve as the sales and customer development process. And the back end, the jails, prisons, probation and parole services provide the products and services. They are with few exceptions factories of despair, people-warehousing, anti-rehabilitation and recidivism. A costly business with lots of repeat customers. And I do recognize a non-effective, monumental waste of money when I see it and I don't like having a country that wins the award for the largest percentage of criminals in the world.

I think it's time we re-evaluate the effectiveness of these programs and the social and monetary costs. Is the objective to lock up as many as possible, or to create a system focused on the root causes, prevention and rehabilitation? What do you think?

Chapter Ten

The Immigration Trick

The immigration trick is complicated and multi-faceted. Some politicians gain political currency by pandering to the anti-immigration crowd while others gain by pandering to the pro-immigration contingent and the undocumented residents. Depending on which side of the fence you're on the trick is to gain your support, and potentially legalize millions of new potential voters. In the end the trick is on the Country. We went through this in the Reagan administration and it was supposed to solve the problem but the government failed to follow through with border protection and other measures, so here we are again with a much bigger issue.

This is a country of immigrants. Although I'm a natural born U.S. citizen, and I suspect President *Obama* is too, my father's parents and his older brother were born in *Norway*. So I'm what they call a second-generation American. Most of our population can trace their roots and generally they're foreign ones. There are very few who can go back several U.S. generations and even fewer who are the descendants of the Pilgrims. Essentially, unless you're *American Indian*, we're all immigrants.

I doubt if many people in this country have an objection to legal immigration, it's the illegal kind that seems to upset people. Most countries enforce their immigration laws. The U.S., on the other hand has a more laissez-faire, perhaps even lackadaisical approach.

The 2010 census reported that approximately 13% of the population is foreign-born, with 7.3% non-citizens. Fifty-three percent come from *Latin America* (over half of those from *Mexico*) and the next largest category originated in *Asian* countries. Government estimates peg the number of illegal immigrants (undocumented) at 11.1 million, 58% of those are from *Mexico*. Before your eyes glaze over with the data, let's look further into the issues.

Enforcement

The first issue is enforcement of our immigration laws. Moves toward stronger enforcement have gained some traction following 9/11. Why don't we enforce the laws? There are several reasons.

First, many citizens don't consider it a problem. Second, it affects the States disproportionately with those bordering *Mexico* experiencing the greatest impact. Third, a traditional demand for "cheap labor." Fourth, it's difficult and costly. Fifth, periodic efforts to limit the problem (by legalizing those already in the country).

And sixth, perhaps most importantly: confusion, lack of will and direction, ineptness, and inertia in the political process.

Some even believe that certain politicians favor either the status quo,
or are maneuvering to gain political advantage through legalization of
millions of potential voters. It's another mess, but we've been through
this before. In fact, we've wrestled with this issue throughout our history.

"Under the *Articles of Confederation* [Enacted in 1781 and Replaced
by the Constitution in 1788], the question of citizenship and the naturalization of immigrants remained with the individual states.
Pennsylvania allowed any foreigner of "good character," who took an
oath of allegiance to the state, to acquire property and after one year's
residency become a citizen entitled to "all the rights of a natural born
subject of this state."

New York followed *Pennsylvania*'s model and added a requirement for
foreigners to renounce all allegiance to any foreign prince. *Maryland*'s
naturalization law required a declaration of "belief in the 'Christian
religion' and an oath of allegiance." In *South Carolina*, full naturalization required "at least two years of residency and a special act of the
legislature." (immigration.procon.org.)

In 1849 the *Supreme Court* ruled that it was the Federal government's
responsibility to regulate immigration.

There is some precedent for believing the notion that government officials legalize immigrants to increase voter registration. In 1868 that's
exactly what happened. As a part of the *Tammany Hall* scandal *Boss
Tweed* arranged to naturalize 20-30,000 Irish immigrants in the six
weeks preceding a *New York* election. It is said one judge processed
10,000 in just two weeks!

In the 1880 to 1924 period the great *European* migration saw an average of 560,000 immigrants per year. Throughout our history there have been exclusions (notably *Chinese*) and restrictions based on country of origin, religion, ethnicity, etc.

There has also been favored treatment (*Europeans, Cubans*, etc.) or exceptions based on special skills or talents or financial investment in the country, etc. Practically any policy you can imagine has been in place at one time or another.

Legalization

In 1986 the largest legalization of illegal immigrants took place. Congress passed SB1200, and *President Reagan* signed it into law, granting amnesty to millions of immigrants who entered the country illegally. This was an easy decision for Reagan. On his radio broadcasts he would say: "An illegal alien is just another willing worker." But to many this represented "failed legislation" because the provisions requiring greater border and employer enforcement efforts were weak and incomplete. As a result we're once again faced with a remarkably similar dilemma.

On a personal note, I recall the huge numbers of "undocumenteds" living in *Los Angeles*. It seemed as though there was rarely any enforcement or deportation. If I had been a *Mexican* without legal papers I certainly wouldn't have worried too much about being deported. And, counterfeit "Green Cards" and *California* Drivers Licenses were readily available in *MacArthur Park* or other convenient locales. It was a business like any other. I also was a frequent visitor to *Mexico*, only about two hours down Interstate 5. I recall the warning signs along the highway. Signs that depicted images of a family holding hands while they ran across the freeway. Signs intended to prevent deaths or injury of these unlawful entrants.

And I remember my reaction, a bittersweet one; sad that people would have to risk their lives to enter *America*, but impressed that the State *Transportation Agency* would maintain these warnings.

While in *Tijuana* I sometimes visited friends who lived in the hills in the North end of town, overlooking the International Border. We would eat barbeque, drink *Tecate* beer and watch the real life drama that played out on the fields along the river beneath us. A "cat and mouse" game between "*La Migra*" (Border Patrol officers) and the "Coyotes" (smugglers of human beings). The Migra would have their pickup trucks and SUV's and the immigrants had nothing but stealth, strategy and fast feet. We would always "root" for the *Mexican* illegals.

Once an illegal made it across the border he was still in danger of apprehension because of more intense law enforcement close to the line, but most would head North anyway, towards *Los Angeles*, or further on to the rich agricultural fields in the *San Joaquin Valley*. Employees seeking work and Americans eager to employ them.

When the new immigrants headed north there was another checkpoint near *San Clemente* (the town where *Richard Nixon* had his "Western White House"). At that checkpoint officers would stop all traffic (or at least slow it down and peer into cars for suspicious people - a form of "profiling"). They would inspect *Greyhound* buses, some trucks and private vehicles. Light-skinned, non-Indian-looking passengers were generally waved through without incident. As a fascinating side note, the State of *California* constructed a roadside public park a short distance south of the Immigration checkpoint. From that vantage point the "Coyotes" escorting their human cargo could, with binoculars or naked-eye, see when the Checkpoint changed shifts or temporarily closed. Then they would quickly hop in their vehicles and promptly drive through without being detected. It was almost as though the State had constructed this convenience to facilitate the transport of undocumented immigrants.

This mega-game of international intrigue continues today.

[97]

Although enforcement has improved and fences constructed or re-paired, the main reason for a smaller number of *Mexican* illegal immigrants is due to the fact that "*Coming to America*" is just not that appealing anymore. The decline in the U.S. economy, the brutality of the drug cartel near the border, improved documentation requirements, and modest enforcement enhancements have all contributed.

The terrorist threat along the southern U.S. border isn't one of my big-gest concerns. I haven't heard of any *Mexican* Terrorists anyway. To me they're not a credible threat to our security. However the possibil-ity of terrorist-inclined individuals sneaking across our southern border is a possibility, although I believe they would rather come in by airplane on a student or visitor visa.

Stepped Up Enforcement

Ironically, the pro-immigration *Obama* administration is deporting people at a higher rate than any previous President. An estimated 2 million people by 2014. Stricter enforcement was already in place dur-ing the *Bush* presidency, but there has been even greater enforcement since then. *Obama* probably isn't happy with this accomplishment; although he emphasizes that the emphasis is on removing criminals. The motivation is undoubtedly a part of the administration's desire to pass comprehensive immigration reform. That plan has been repeated-ly rejected by Congress because they questioned the Executive Branch's commitment to enforcement.

As a side-note even those who have been deported may benefit from their stay in the United States. American companies are busy relocat-ing pieces of their high cost U.S. based customer service operations to *Mexico* to take advantage of the lower labor costs (approx. $4/hr USD). Deportees are prime employee prospects as they are better able to relate to *American* customers and have some English-language flu-ency. *Time-Warner*, *Best Buy*, and *Dish Network* are some of the companies trying this approach.

[98]

The burgeoning Mexico-based call centers have expanded over 100% in just the three years from 2007-2010, totaling an astounding 18,701 locations.

A Conundrum

What should we do? Well, something is better than nothing! Instead of having millions of illegals ("undocumented[s]" if you prefer) why not legalize them? Of course the fiscal impact, especially on entitlement programs, the labor market, unemployment, *Social Security*, etc, is an essential part of any analysis of an amnesty/legalization proposal as are the issues of border and visa security. However, it is a problem that needs to be dealt with. Get them (undocumenteds) out of the underground economy and into a path to citizenship. Repatriate the criminals. Tighten the borders. Make it clear we'll never do it again. Start respecting our laws and our country.

Ancient Rome declined because it had a Senate,
now what's going to happen to us
with both a House and a Senate?

-Will Rogers

The less government interferes with private pursuits,
the better for general prosperity.

--Martin Van Buren

The seed of revolution is repression.

--Woodrow Wilson

America does not go abroad in search of monsters to
destroy.

--John Quincy Adams

Chapter Eleven

The Tax Trick

The trick here is to get you to pay taxes while the corporations and the wealthy pay little or none. The other trick is to confuse the heck out of you. The tax laws are overly complex, unfair, and the result of thousands of deals, lobbying efforts, and special interests. The system doesn't provide sufficient revenue to fund the government and is a monumental irritant for millions of people.

The constant manipulation of tax laws is designed to benefit the interests of a few. Although *Personal Income Taxes* represent the largest source of revenue for our federal government the corporations and the wealthy can legally avoid most, if not all of these assessments. Various loopholes, passive income provisions, obscure credits, and other *CPA*, and tax attorney inspired benefits favor those who have the most influence and wealth. The tax laws are designed for them, not you and I. They have powerful lobbyists to ensure their "special interests" are protected. And they have the best legal and accounting talent. When I was living in *California* I was paying the State Income Tax of almost 10%, Federal Income Tax of 38%, Sales Tax of 7%, Fuel (gasoline tax) of 37.5 cents per gallon, property tax, telephone taxes, etc. When you include less obvious taxes like excise taxes, luxury taxes, utility taxes, inheritance taxes, etc., it makes a flat rate tax or consumption tax look pretty good.

[101]

Our tax rates may not be the highest in the world, but the ingeniousness and variety of them certainly place the uninformed or those without access to this type of expertise at considerable disadvantage.

A Variety of Taxes

There is an incredible array of taxes in this country. Generally we fail to think about all of the ways, and how frequently the Government has their hands in our wallets. On the previous page I itemized some of the taxes I paid a few years ago. But there are many more. Hidden taxes, taxes on top of taxes, taxes for everything you can imagine and taxes in a few areas you may not.

Taxes don't die easily; perhaps the best example of this phenomenon is 3% tax on long distance telephone calls created in 1898 to partially finance the *Spanish-American War*. When the tax was imposed it was designed to be a tax on the wealthy as only the rich had telephones at the end of the 19th century. The Appeals Court struck down the tax in 2006 after the *Treasury Department* tried unsuccessfully to keep it in effect. It finally was discontinued after 108 years!

Below, I have listed some examples of common taxes, fees and charges you may pay to the Government. Hopefully you won't encounter all of them this year, but it's likely you'll be subject to most, if not all, over the course of a lifetime. Remember, this is only a partial list!

Examples of Common Taxes

Accounts Receivable Tax, Building Permit Tax, Capital Gains Tax, license Tax, Cigarette Tax, Corporate Income Tax, Court Fines (indirect taxes), Dog License Tax, Drivers License Tax, Federal Income Tax, Federal Unemployment Tax, Fishing License Tax, Food License Tax, Fuel permit tax, Gasoline Tax, Hunting License Tax, Inheritance Tax, State Income Tax, Inventory tax, IRS Interest Charges or IRS Penalties, Liquor Tax, Local Income Tax, Luxury Taxes, Marriage License Tax, Medicare Tax, Obamacare Tax & penalties, Property Tax, Real Estate Tax, Septic Permit Tax, Service Charge Taxes, Social Security Tax, Road Usage Taxes, Sales Taxes, Recreational Vehicle Tax, Toll Booth Taxes, School Tax, State Income Tax, State Unemployment Tax, Telephone federal excise tax, Telephone federal universal service fee tax, Telephone federal, state and local surcharge taxes, Telephone minimum usage surcharge tax, Telephone recurring and non-recurring charges tax, Telephone state and local tax, Telephone usage charge tax, Toll Bridge Taxes, Toll Road Taxes, Toll Tunnel Taxes, Traffic Fines/Court fees, Trailer Registration Tax, Utility Taxes, Vehicle License Registration Tax, Vehicle Sales Tax, Watercraft Registration Tax, Well Permit Tax, Workers Compensation Tax, etc.

It is difficult to definitively ascertain who pays U.S. income tax. As the complexities of the tax laws can result in someone making $30,000 paying more federal income tax than someone making $250,000 a year. Therefore the data is expressed in "averages" supposedly representing the typical taxpayer within a specific "bracket."

Who Pays the most Taxes?

- The lowest 20% of earners (who average about $12,400 per year) paid 16.0% of their income to various forms of taxes in 2009
- The next 20% (about $25,000/year) paid 20.5% in taxes
- The middle 20% (about $33,400/year) paid 25.3% in taxes
- The next 20%, (about $66,000/year) paid 28.5% in taxes
- The next 10%, (about $100,000/year) paid 30.2% in taxes
- The next 5% ($141,000/year) paid 31.2% in taxes
- The next 4% ($245,000/year) paid 31.6% in taxes
- The top 1% (those who take in $1.3 million per year on average) paid 30.8% of their income to taxes

Source: truthfulpolitics.com

Our Friends at the IRS

Perhaps the most feared government agency is the *IRS*. This agency is the government's designated "collection agent."

Many average citizens believe that they could be targeted for special scrutiny or audits. That they could end up on some "enemies" list or worse. We all know this abuse of authority and impartiality has occurred to others.

The 2012 scandal involving barriers or delays for groups and organizations seeking tax exempt, non-profit status is a case in point. In this instance, organizations thought to be affiliated with the "Tea Party" were not treated fairly by the government apparently for political reasons.

Because the *Democratic Party* was in control, the bureaucrats thought they could "punish"/disadvantage conservative, *Republican Tea Party* affiliated organizations. This is incredible, although probably not rare. Government agencies can turn rogue and often do.

Favorable treatment can be given to organizations or individuals aligned or supportive of the political party in power. It is good that these examples of politically motivated *IRS* harassment surfaced for all to see.

Although the *IRS* acknowledged improprieties, they have, according to the *Washington Post*, apparently stymied Congressional investigators by slowly providing heavily redacted documents to Congressional Committee members. *IRS* officials maintain that the unfair practices were not widespread and initiated by regional managers, not from *Washington* headquarters. As a side-note, world renowned neurosurgeon and conservative spokesman *Dr. Ben Carson* (not me, but I like the name) told the *Washington Times* (Oct. 3, 2013) that he believed the *IRS* audited him in retribution for remarks he made critical of the *Obama* administration at a Prayer Breakfast a few months earlier. And *President Obama* was present. Of course the good doctor could be wrong, it might just be coincidence. Although he had never been audited prior to that.

Should you be concerned that you too might be scrutinized or harassed by *IRS* government agents for your expressed political opinions? You decide.

Our Amazing Tax System

Do we need an entirely different tax system? Are the 73,000 pages of the tax code indicative of a fair, easily understood system or one that should be junked?

If the system annually drains billions of hours out of the productive economy, requires millions of tax preparers, tens of thousands of tax attorneys, tens of thousands of IRS employees, and still is incomprehensible it may be time to start over.

What would work? What would be fair? A national sales tax, a Value Added Tax, flat tax, consumption tax?

Sarah Keller and *Deborah Schanz* are *German* economists whose research into taxation is widely respected. According to *Forbes* Magazine on their "Tax Attractiveness Index" the U.S. tax system ranks 94th out of 100, just below *Zimbabwe*, (although we did beat out *Venezuela*).

The authors view taxation from a strategic perspective. In a globalized economy they believe a strategic tax system will attract companies, investment and jobs. The researchers objectified their assessment by determining sixteen separate indices for international comparison. Not surprisingly offshore tax haven countries, e.g. *Bermuda*, *Bahamas*, *Cayman Islands*, rank highly. Regionally *Caribbean* countries rank highest, followed by *Europe*, the *Middle East* and *Africa*; the *Americas* and *Asia* bringing up the bottom.

The main point, again, is we need to view our tax system as a strategic and competitive advantage or disadvantage (and not a special interest wealth transfer system).

This is the way wealthy people look at it, from an international perspective. And, as you may be aware because of the tax system's long reach, they can't escape it completely by moving abroad. Accordingly, there has been a recent surge in American foreign residents giving up their U.S. citizenship for taxation reasons.

The Tax Game

Meanwhile certain U.S. Corporations have become particularly skillful at avoiding or evading income tax. *GE* is the undisputed champion of avoiding paying income tax, but there are many others.

An *MSNBC* analysis of corporate tax cheats (as reported by Alternet.org) include: 1) *Google*, 2) *NewsCorp*, 3) *Boeing*, 4) *Pfizer*, 5) *Oracle*, 6) *Altria* (*Phillip Morris*), 7) *IBM*, 8) *Time-Warner*, 9) *Morgan-Stanley*, 10) *Microsoft*.

Some of the most common ways these corporations avoid taxes are through the use of: tax shelters, tax havens, offshore investments, foreign subsidiaries, etc. I'm all for corporations and individuals legally minimizing their tax liabilities, but not when it involves such blatant tactics resulting in loss of U.S. jobs and investment or transfer of tax burden to others. However, should we be blaming the corporate giants or their enabler, the Government? Actually, it is the result of major campaign contributions, aggressive lobbying, sponsored tax code revisions and other interesting strategies.

As a result of our crazy tax structure most corporate growth is not helping America. Although the intellectual property may be owned by a U.S. corporation the production entities are generally offshore. These profitable subsidiaries are in countries with cheaper labor and avoid U.S. taxes. So if the jobs and profit are overseas where's the benefit? It's as though our tricky politicians in collusion with profit-hungry major corporations have conspired to weaken the U.S. economy. It may not be treasonous but it's certainly unfair, not in the best interests of the majority, and questionable from an ethical standpoint.

Taxes and the Rich

We all know the income tax system is unfair—it favors the wealthy. Perhaps you are familiar with the saying: "The poor pay more!" And they do. In poor neighborhoods the cost of living is not low.

[107]

Groceries cost more, insurance is higher; there are Check Cashing stores instead of banks. Everything is expensive. They don't locate *Costco*'s in underprivileged ghettos— it's more like "Joe's Corner Market," or "Pepe's Liquor," with low quality merchandise and high price tags. But the poor don't pay the most in income tax, (only 42% of Americans pay any income tax at all) although they do pay disproportionately more in sales tax, the most regressive tax, primarily because a higher percentage of their income is spent on consumables.

Although the uber-wealthy may pay substantial dollars in income tax they don't pay a high percentage. First, the tax laws were written for them. Second, they have access to "creative accounting." Third, much of their income comes from "capital gains." Finally, they have infinitely more places to stash, hide, invest or park money, including offshore tax havens.

It's the middle-class that's really screwed under our tax system. They're not poor enough to avoid income tax altogether and not rich enough to enjoy all the loopholes and preferential treatment. Our tax system should really be called a "Wealth Re-distribution System," with money transferred to the rich and the poor. In a sense it has become a quasi-welfare program benefitting those on the extremes. Welfare for the rich and the poor. What a system!

Under current law and with certain family composition and income circumstances the poor become eligible for tax credits to the extent that they can often receive more in refunds than they paid in taxes. In some cases much more. In other cases nothing is paid yet individuals and families can claim credits and "refunds."

My favorite billionaire is *Warren Buffet*. I had the opportunity to meet him once at a presentation he made to a group at the *California Institute of Technology*. He's "sharp as a tack," exceptionally well-informed, and "down to earth" with folksy humor, and a disarming air of humility.

Mr. Buffet is an outspoken critic of our current tax system and an advocate for reform. As one of the world's wealthiest individuals he has considerable insight into the economic and taxation systems.

In a (Nov. 25th) 2012 op-ed article in the *New York Times* the investor-tycoon advocated for higher taxes on the wealthy. And he's expressed this position on many occasions. (He's fond of saying his not-overly-highly-compensated Secretary pays a higher marginal tax rate than he does!) In the article he recites the history of taxes on Capital Gains, the kind of passive income investments which the wealthy prefer because of their favorable tax treatment, and marginal rates on dividends. He refers to the *Forbes 400*, the wealthiest individuals in *America* and the fact that they have $1.7 *trillion* to invest.

He reported the ultra wealthy had an average (2009) income of $202 million-- "which works out to a 'wage' of $97,000 per hour, based on a 40 hour workweek." (Wouldn't you like to earn just a few hundred an hour?) He went on to say that more than a quarter of these ultra-wealthy "paid less than 15%...in combined federal income and payroll taxes"...and..."a few actually paid nothing." Buffet went on to advocate for a "minimum tax on high incomes." His proposal is 30% of taxable income on income "between 1 million and $10 million," and "35% above that." His plan makes sense and he goes on to support it further by adding: "A plain and simple rule like that will block the efforts of lobbyists, lawyers, and contribution-hungry legislators to keep the ultra-rich paying rates well below those incurred by people with income just a tiny fraction of ours (sic)."

You gotta love *Buffet*! He tells it like it is! And he's not so greedy and selfish that he doesn't have empathy for those at the lower rungs of the economic ladder. An uber-tycoon with compassion!

As evidence of that concern his plan is to donate the bulk of his fortune to charity; most of it to his friends *Bill and Melinda Gates'* Foundation.

Death Tax

The Estate Tax is sometimes referred to as a "death tax." We've all heard the saying attributed to *Ben Franklin*: "...in this world nothing can be said to be certain, except death and taxes."

Well, death may be certain but a death tax is not. In fact, according to an article at the *Center on Budget Policy and Programs* currently only individual estates valued at $5.25m or more or $10.5m for married couples are taxed by the government. The exempt amount has quad-rupled since 2001 and only 0.14%; or about 2 out of 1,000 of all estates meet these criteria. And, estate planning and a knowledgeable attorney can avoid all or most of these levies. The ceiling is so high and the exemptions so generous that only 20 family owned businesses or farms will pay any taxes whatsoever in 2013, and they will average only 4.9%. ("Myths and Realities about the Estate Tax," Huang & Frentz, 8/29/13).

Although I'm opposed to most taxes the value of these estates have typically increased, partially as a consequence of favorable capital gains exemptions for years, and if the assets were sold there would be taxable income. It's not an insignificant source of income for the Government. If the tax was eliminated it would cost $200 billion over the next ten years, and if the tax was increased to levels in place prior to the Bush tax cuts it would add about $750 billion in revenue.

How we Compare

Conservative politicians and the wealthy would have you believe that the U.S. is the most heavily taxed country in the world. Liberal politi-cians and organizations would say the opposite. But actually we come out about in the middle and generally lower than other highly devel-oped nations. The *Tax Foundation* (www.taxfoundation.org) analyzed *OCED* data to ascertain which countries have the most progressive tax systems. What they discovered may surprise you.

According to the *Tax Foundation* only in *Italy* and the United States do the top ten percent of households pay more than 40% of the total tax burden. In the U.S. it's 45.1% (and in *Italy* 42.2%). Here's some more: *Australia* 36.8%, *Canada* 35.8%, *Denmark* 26.2%, *France* 28.0%, *Germany* 31.2%, *Ireland* 39.1%, *Japan* 28.5%, *U.K.* 38.6%. Now, you will note these figures are at odds with the data compiled by "truthfulpolitics.com (reported a few pages earlier). So who's right? If I had to decide, I'd say neither.

A name like *"truthful politics"* although the site looks legit sounds like an oxymoron and the *"Tax Foundation"* probably has an axe to grind, too— it was founded and supported by big business and conservative interests. So I went to the source of international data and checked out *tax rates* compiled by *OECD*. When doing research it's important to value objectivity, reliability, and validity. In politics and money those qualities are hard to find. The *OECD* data places the U.S. about in the middle of developed countries with a 35% Marginal Tax Rate (rate applied to the highest income bracket). Their methodology appears fair, but if you want to check it out be my guest; the analysis I used can be found in *Global Finance Magazine* (Global Database *at www.gfmag.com*). "In 2012, *Aruba* had the world's highest top marginal rate, 59%, followed by *Sweden*, 56.6%, and *Denmark*, 55.4%. At the other end of the spectrum, besides a handful of countries that do not have personal income taxes, *Macedonia*, *Bulgaria*, *Albania* and *Bosnia-Herzegovina* all showed the lowest top marginal rate, 10%."

It should be noted that for seventeen years (1965-1981) the U.S. had a top marginal tax rate of 70%(!), - in the 1950's it was 92%(!) - although in all probability nobody ever paid top rates due to tax breaks and deductions. I selected a few more countries for comparison:

France: 45%	China: 45%
Brazil: 27.5%	Japan: 50%
Germany: 45%	India: 30%
U.K: 50%	USA: 35%

It appears the U.S. is competitive and even has some "wiggle" room. Although we're a little higher than the *OECD* 28.9% average for all nations, we're somewhat below the western *European* and *Asian* nations we typically use as benchmark comparatives.

Unfair?

A fair tax is another oxymoron. Taxes are designed to support the government, achieve economic advantage, political objectives and social purpose. Countries are constantly manipulating rates and tax targets to maintain competitive advantage while satisfying fiscal needs.

President Kennedy understood the tax dilemma when he said: "It is a paradoxical truth that tax rates are too high today and tax revenues are too low and the soundest way to raise the revenues in the long run is to cut the tax rates.... [A]n economy constrained by high tax rates will never produce enough revenue to balance the budget, just as it will never create enough jobs or enough profits." But as appealing as this logic is, it is difficult to translate into tax law. There are many other elements in play, not the least of which is the ever-increasing scope and expense of government. It never seems to balance out and there's this constant tug-of-war. The deck unfortunately, is stacked in favor of those with the most political clout.

If you were donating big bucks to key political leaders do you think you might be able to get more tax-breaks than the average schmuck? Do you believe you would have to pay your "fair share?"

Of course not. It's all a trick, orchestrated by those who have the most, and executed by the easily bought politicians. And because so many of our politicians are also wealthy, they are the beneficiaries of the very tax loopholes they promote.

Do You Hate Taxes?

According to a (April 16, 2013) *New York Times* article, in 75 years of surveys no more than a "tiny percentage of Americans said the amount they paid in taxes was too low." And the biggest dissatisfaction is not with paying taxes but with the system's complexity and government waste. 70-80% of taxpayers believe the government "wastes a lot of money." And although almost everyone hates taxes, *Republicans* and high earners hate taxes more than *Democrats* and those in lower brackets.

A Futuristic Tax System

Our tax system is antiquated, overly cumbersome and complex and not helping us in this fast-changing economic climate. It needs to be re-thought and re-designed. The current model should be junked and replaced with one better suited for current realities and future possi-bilities. The system should be strategic. A tax system that advances our competitiveness, builds our economy, attracts wealth and invest-ment. It should promote employment rather than rewarding transfer of productive capacity and jobs offshore. It should be instrumental in moving people from dependence to independence.

Instead of endlessly pursuing tricks and games to assist business in avoiding tax levies the Government should re-focus on developing a fair, easily understood system, one that clearly demonstrates purpose-fulness, societal strengthening, and promotion of joint objectives. We should learn from our mistakes and from the errors and successes of competitor nations. Let's face it that's what they are: the competition. And, our tax system should be one more tool in our arsenal of interna-tional economic competitive advantage.

*Render therefore unto Caesar
the things which are Caesar's;
and unto God the things that are God's.*

*--The Holy Bible, King James version,
Matthew 22:20-22*

*I may be president of the United States, but my private
life is nobody's damned business.*

--Chester A. Arthur

*Democracy... while it lasts is more bloody
than either aristocracy or monarchy.
Remember, democracy never lasts long.
It soon wastes, exhausts, and murders itself.
There is never a democracy that did not commit
suicide.*

--John Adams

Chapter Twelve

The Misinformation Trick

Providing you with slanted, biased, misleading or downright bad information is a government art-form. People generally view data as the truth and statistics as mathematical certainty. The trick is to get you to believe it so that you will feel better about yourself, your country, or the party in power. The motives are: To gain political support for candidates, officeholders, parties, positions or programs; and/or to put the opposition in bad light.

Does anyone trust government statistics? Do you? Probably not; and with good reason. There's a classic book: *"How to Lie with Statistics"*— it should be a government publication. The government doesn't want an informed populous or electorate. To the contrary, they want a misinformed public, albeit a supportive one. Administrations want a public that feels prosperous and happy. And they want you to believe that they're responsible for these good times. And what if times aren't good? That doesn't mean that they can't be portrayed in a more favorable light.

Go Figure Unemployment

If you don't believe the unemployment rate, raise your hand! I don't see any hands up in the air. That must mean everyone believes the unemployment rate. See, I tricked you! And so does the government.

[115]

To continue examining the unemployment rate; at the time this is being written the officially reported rate is about seven-and-one-half percent. The real rate (using the formula from the 1960's) is about twice the current official rate.

The government uses various indices and formulas termed U-1 through U-6. The "official" rate currently uses U-3. People counted as unemployed are:

- Not Self-Employed;
- 16 Years of Age Or Older;
- Without a job;
- Currently available for work; and,
- Have actively looked for work in the prior four weeks.

Your government has an interesting methodology for ascertaining the number of unemployed. Instead of using actual payroll data they survey over 60,000 households monthly and weigh the results demographically. The "labor force" is defined as the number of people who are actively working jobs plus the number of people who are available for work. They subtract people in categories such as: "discouraged" workers (i.e., stopped looking for work), military personnel, students (returning to school), prisoners, etc. Interestingly, much of the "improvement" in the jobless rate is due to the shrinkage of the American workforce, primarily as a result of discouraged workers ceasing their efforts to find a job. They're still unemployed, but not counted as such. The other big problem centers around those *involuntarily* working part-time. They're considered employed although they're not fully employed. In June, 2013 the government calculated the U-6 unemployment rate at 14.3% and the "official" (U-3) rate was 7.6%. What a cruel joke.

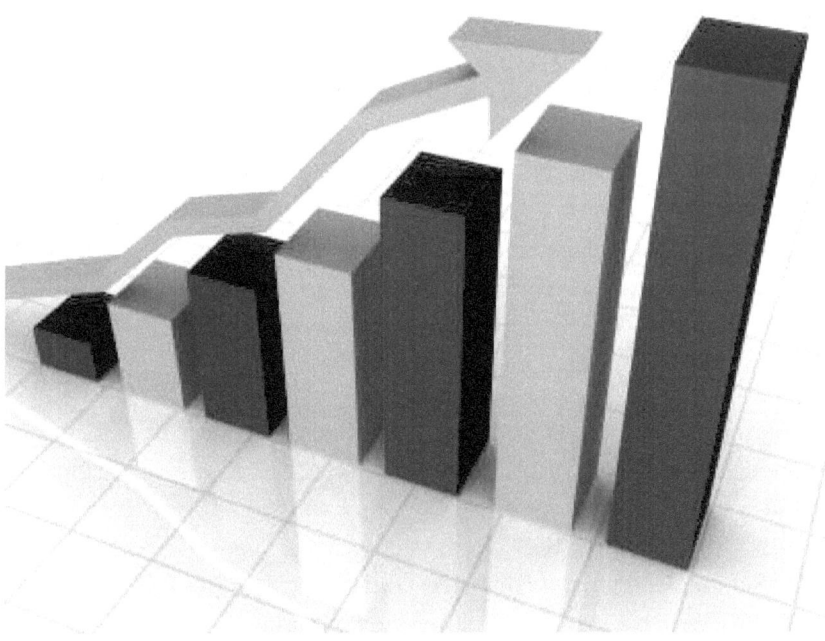

Like Blowing Up a Balloon

Inflation is another number the government likes to play with. It's important because the rate of inflation translates into the Cost of Living, and it is linked to many other programs such as the granddaddy of them all-- *Social Security*. Public and private sector pay raises and pension increases are impacted by this number. And your sense of well-being is too. The government prefers to have some inflation; it results in asset appreciation and a sense of well-being, as long as it's kept in check.

Low cost credit, mortgages, business loans, etc, are stimulating to our economy and healthy growth. Major, or runaway inflation such as in in the early 1920's in *Germany*, 1975-1991 in *Argentina*, 1990-1991 in *Brazil*, or other nations can be disastrous.

Perhaps the most infamous, extreme and recent example of out-of-control inflation occurred in *Zimbabwe* in the first decade of the twenty-first century (until 2009) when the official currency was replaced every few weeks with larger denominations, prices increased hourly, and shortly before the collapse a *hundred trillion dollars* would buy a cup of coffee! I have several of these *Trillion Dollar* banknotes notes as a conversation piece and I've been known to casually give a hundred trillion to my grateful friends or to a coffee shop waitress. (Interestingly, these banknotes now cost more as collector's items than they were worth when they were legitimate currency in circulation.)

Runaway inflation has occurred many times in the past and it will happen again. Obviously, your government has a consuming interest in how inflation is reported.

As Senior Economist *John Tanny* (RealClearMarkets) said in *Vanderbilt Business* magazine: "Rather than clinging to the *CPI* as false evidence of light inflation, and worse, targeting consumer prices, monetary authorities should instead target a stable gold price with an eye on bringing it down substantially."

The *Vanderbilt* study reports: "In order to measure general price increases, the *Bureau of Labor Statistics* constructs an imaginary "market basket" of goods that an average family needs to lead an average life. The market basket includes *specific* items relating to housing, food, transportation, medical care, clothing, entertainment, education and communication. Currently, there are approximately 80,000 items in the 'basket.' Price data for these items is collected monthly from 22,500 specific outlets and 7,300 specific housing units in 44 urban areas. The prices for identical goods from the same area are averaged, and individual price indices are calculated for each item and geographic area. Finally the individual price indices are in essence summed up to create the "price" of the entire market basket. The final price is actually a weighted sum, the weights reflecting the proportion that the average family spends on various categories and the population of the geographic area."

There's another problem with the government's methodology. Who's average? If you live further from work you spend more on transportation, if you're on a special diet your food costs are different; if you're atypical in any significant way you may be in trouble. Plus, if you're on *Social Security* you're stuck with a nationwide *CPI* to calculate your monthly pension.

In 1962 a *Hershey Bar* cost a nickel, *U.S. postage* was 4 cents, a *McDonald's* hamburger cost 28 cents, a gallon of gasoline was 31 cents, and a new *Chevrolet* was $2,529. Many of these items have seen price increases of well over 1,000%. But then, your salary probably has too! The problem, of course, is these increases disproportionately hit the poor. And, more of us are poor. Even middle-class wages have stagnated since 1998.

The government seems to play games with practically all data, reports and information. This is natural, and a common practice. Corporations are good at it, but the government is a Master!

The message: Don't believe government reports and official statistics, they're manipulated, designed to make you feel better, and rooted in deception and fantasy.

OUT TO GET YOU

The happiness of society is the end of government.

--John Adams

*It's no exaggeration to say that the undecideds could go
one way or another.*

--George H. W. Bush

*To live under the American Constitution is the greatest
political privilege that was ever accorded
to the human race.*

--Calvin Coolidge

*A government big enough to give you everything you
want
is a government big enough to take from you everything
you have.*

--Gerald R. Ford

[120]

Chapter Thirteen

The "Spin" Trick

This trick is a powerful one and related to the misinformation trick. The objective is to take a piece of news or information and twist it with clever rhetoric. Most often applied to unfavorable situations or bad news, the technique is to put a "pretty face" on it; a negative that can be turned into a positive.

Rahm Emanuel is the Mayor of *Chicago*. He's a politician. Before becoming Mr. Mayor he was *President Obama*'s Chief of Staff. In that role he was quoted as saying: *"You never let a serious crisis go to waste."* He went on to say: "What I mean by that, it's an opportunity to do things you think you could not do before."

If you were ever suspicious about political motivations before reading that quote consider your suspicions confirmed! It reminds me of the Chinese "Yin-Yang" which in Eastern philosophy has been interpreted to mean crisis and opportunity. However, the application of this principle in politics is more cynical. It is most often used to divert the public's attention, to garner support for new spending initiatives, or to gain political advantage. Masterful politicians can subvert the public's interests and obtain leverage in times of crisis particularly if they can tap into public fear or emotion.

A recent example is the tragic death of a young man named *Trayvon Martin*. This horrible event captured the public's attention in mid-2013 and diverted us from focusing on the *Benghazi* debacle, the *IRS* "*Tea Party*" scandal, the healthcare controversy, the massive spying by U.S. officials on our allies and citizens, the expanding conflict in *Syria*, etc. *President Obama* identified with young Mr. *Martin* saying first "if I had a son he would look like *Trayvon*," and later "*Trayvon* could have been me." While there's some truth here and politicians may have genuine concern and sincere empathy they certainly can be adroit at turning current news events into a personal or public political advantage.

The "Unbiased" Media

The spin trick has expanded to include the media who increasingly rely on government data and information to supply their listeners, viewers, and readers. As investigative reporting has waned government propaganda has expanded. (Whenever there's a vacuum, something will arrive to fill it.) Furthermore, the personal views of reporters seem to increasingly contaminate their reporting. And, media management frequently has an agenda as well, if it's labeled as such that's fine, but more often than not, it isn't.

I thoroughly enjoy the book *Freakonomics* by *Steven D. Levitt* and *Stephen J. Dubner*. They expose the *"The Hidden Side of Everything"* and *Dubner* has a website that does the same. On Feb. 16, 2012 he reported the following study.

Here's how 20 major media outlets rank on Groseclose and Milyo's slant scale, with 100 representing the most liberal and zero the most conservative:

ABC Good Morning America	56.1
ABC World News Tonight	61.0
CBS Early Show	66.6
CBS Evening News	73.7
CNN NewsNight with/Aaron Brown	56.0
Drudge Report	60.4
Fox News Spec. Rept. w/Brit Hume	39.7
Los Angeles Times	70.0
NBC Nightly News	61.6
NBC Today Show	64.0
New York Times	73.7
Newshour with Jim Lehrer	55.8
Newsweek	66.3
NPR Morning Edition	66.3
Time Magazine	65.4
U.S. News and World Report	65.8
USA Today	63.4
Wall Street Journal	85.1
Washington Post	66.6
Washington Times	35.4

There are some surprises on that list and it challenges our thinking. For example: The *Wall Street Journal*, reporting on that bastion of capitalism, the investment and finance communities, scored incredibly high on the liberal side. Go figure. (Conservative *Rupert Murdoch* owns corporations which in turn own both the *Wall Street Journal* and *Fox News*.) Of course the *Washington Times*, previously owned by *Rev. Sun Moon* and the *Unification Church*, has a very conservative pedigree and appropriately scored very low on the liberal scale.

[123]

The point is, if you think you're getting the news - you're right! And if you believe it's unbiased - you're wrong! It helps to be aware of bias and/or "spin" in forming your objective - or subjective - opinion.

Non-Mainstream Media

The Internet has caused extreme consternation to our political leaders. There are two management priorities for politicians: 1) Managing elections, and 2) Managing the media. That's why they spend so much energy cultivating relationships with correspondents, reporters and their networks and news outlets. It's more than spin; it's a form of image management. But with thousands of rogue news sources (blogs, alternative news, scandal and specialty sites) it is an impossible task.

The most controversial and successful example of a rouge Internet source is *Wikileaks*, a news site inaugurated in 2006 by *Julian Assange*. *Wikileaks* turned political news reporting on its ear. *Wikileaks* (wikileaks.org) specializes in publishing news leaks, scandals, secret information, and classified government documents provided by anonymous contributors. It has definitely proved to be an embarrassment (or worse) to many governments (especially ours), corporations, organizations and leaders and led to intimidation and legal problems for its founder.

Can A Leopard Change Its Spots?

Accept the fact that politicians are going to lie, try and get you to support their projects, programs and administrations by using media manipulation techniques. And the media, and individual networks, stations and commentators have their company, professional and personal biases and alliances. This may never change, but you can change your attitude and behaviors to gain multiple perspectives of an issue and to recognize the biases extant. And of course you can expand your perspectives by accessing alternative news sources.

Chapter Fourteen

Terrorism and Foreign Policy Tricks

FEAR. That's what these tricks are all about. We're often mistrustful of other countries and cultures. This fear can be leveraged into programs and funding and a favorable view of the government for protecting us from danger. It can also be used as a rationale for spying on our own citizens and allies and for stripping us of individual freedoms.

These two tricks are combined into this chapter because they are increasingly related. We brand nations terrorist states, terrorist nations or sponsors of terrorism. Our foreign policy has increasingly become governed by risk-perception, risk-assessment and risk-reduction as it pertains to threats of terrorism.

The Terrorism Trick

Terrorism is a real concern. It's always been one, but the escalation in this century has been nothing short of, well, terrifying. The nine-eleven attack on the *World Trade Center* in *New York* alerted all to the very real danger and set a huge government anti-terrorism machinery into operation. The government has since then exploited our fears to gain money and power.

[125]

We've become accustomed to the intrusions into personal privacy and the erosion of freedom which have accompanied the "war on terrorism." And it seems, in substantial measure, to be working.

However, this is definitely not a new trick. The government has been using threats and enemies for years as political and social leverage. One of the most famous, onerous and long-lasting scares was the anti-communism movement spearheaded by Congressman *Joseph McCarthy* and for years working as an arm of the government and using its considerable resources to investigate suspected traitors, spies and alleged Communists. This effort in one form or another lasted from 1947 to 1975. When it began it was called the *House on Un-American Activities Committee* (*Richard Nixon* was a member). In the 1940's and 50's they concentrated on investigating high profile individuals including numerous *Hollywood* stars, directors, executives and writers. While many cooperated with the committee others pled the *"Fifth"* (the self-incrimination protection of the Fifth Amendment of the Constitution). Still others, among them brave individuals, risked their freedom by challenging the government and denouncing the investigation itself as un-American. The "Hollywood Ten" as they became to be referred to were sentenced to fines *and a year in prison*. The whole spectacle was disgusting and embarrassed or ruined the careers of many people. Because *McCarthy* believed that "Negroes" and "Homosexuals" were more susceptible to anti-American activities the committee also targeted members of those groups.

You may know of some of the people whose loyalties were questioned or who were coerced to report others. Among them are: *Ayn Rand, Humphrey Bogart, Arthur Miller, Charlie Chaplin, Lucille Ball, Dalton Trumbo, James Cagney, Orson Bean, Fredric March, Paul Robeson, Zero Mostel, and Orson Wells.*

While some questioned or rallied against the process others used it to attack enemies, gain favor; or in the case of *Walt Disney*, to break a cartoonist and illustrator strike by purchasing a full page ad in *Variety*, blaming Communist agitation for the work action.

[126]

Again, in the 1960's and '70's the Government ramped up its spy network to begin telephone conversation eavesdropping on anti-*Vietnam War* figures such as *Muhammad Ali* (aka *Cassius Clay*), *Martin Luther King, Jane Fonda and Stokley Carmichael.* Illegal wiretapping and surveillance tactics were employed.

It is important to recognize how precarious the freedoms we take for granted are, and the importance of standing up for our rights and the rights of others whose loyalties are called into question.

There is always someone or some group to view as an enemy or to blame for our personal problems or the problems confronting the country. Finding scapegoats is a common pursuit. In *World War II,* we herded *Japanese-Americans* into relocation camps, during the Red Scare we searched for Communist-sympathizers, during the *Vietnam War Asians* were again regarded with suspicion and now it's the *Muslims.*

Terrorism is Real and Freedom is Fragile

The current emphasis on preventing terrorism is of course essential. However, if it means sacrificing our *Constitutional Rights* and inherent freedoms it may not be worth it. Some will argue the effort has been remarkably successful. We still have the occasional attack such as the tragic 2012 *Boston Marathon* incident, but remember immediately following 9/11 when we worried these attacks would be everyday occurrences?

The overall problem is not limited to the containment and reduction of terrorism; it's the accompanying erosion of personal rights and freedoms. This has been the real cost of the war on terrorism. Just look at the changes we've experienced since 2001.

First, the *Homeland Security* and *National Security Agencies*. They installed protections at the airports, undoubtedly a good thing, but they can't "profile" so the harassment of wheelchair-bound grandmothers and small children continues. Importantly the protection from unreasonable searches, the expectation of privacy in telephone and internet conversations and activities, have been sacrificed. And the targeting of "suspicious characters" especially among government employees has been promoted. We've become a nation of snoops and spies and tattle-tales and I don't like it.

In Miami there are many *Cuban* exiles, these types of activities are what they sought to escape. They tell me neighbors would report neighbors or friends, something akin to the experience in *China*, or cold war Communist *Russia*. I frequently have breakfast at a neighborhood *Cuban* Restaurant, there's a sweet grandmotherly type who works there and I always give her a big hug. One day I was talking to her in my "pigeon Spanish" and she commented: "It's getting more and more like *Cuba*, the government controls everything. Communism is why we left!"

Here's a partial list of some of the other important changes since 9/11: Warrantless wiretapping; government sponsored torture, kidnapping and detention; creation of a surveillance society; installation and abuse of the *Patriot Act* (both citizens and immigrants); improper jailing (without charges); government secrecy; "no-fly" lists; political spying; abuse of the *material witness statute*; curtailment of academic freedom; expansion of the *Military Commissions Act*.

As Professor *Gary Orfield* of the *UCLA Civil Rights Project* wrote: "The loss of civil rights often begins with the reduction of rights in a time of crisis, for a minority that has become the scapegoat for a problem facing the nation. The situation can become particularly explosive in a time of national tragedy or war. But when civil rights for one group of Americans are threatened and the disappearance of those rights is accepted, it becomes a potential threat to many others."

According to *nationalpriorities.org* the U.S. has spent almost three-quarters of a trillion dollars on Homeland Security since 2001.

As a side-note, while it costs $40,000-50,000 a year to house and feed domestic criminals, according to a Congressional study reported in the *Miami Herald* (7/31/13) it costs a whopping $2.7 million dollars a year per prisoner at Guantanamo Bay! Yes, everything connected with terrorism seems exorbitantly costly. But your government relies on our fears to further its anti-terrorism agenda. Your tax dollars at work!

A Man Named Snowden

A young man named *Edward Snowden* fled to Hong Kong, then Russia where he was offered asylum over the strenuous objections of the U.S. government. As this is being written he is still in Russia but seeking sanctuary elsewhere. What did *Snowden* do? U.S. officials claim he's a traitor because he divulged government spying secrets he learned while working for the *NSA* (*National Security Agency*) as an independent contractor as well as for the *CIA*. He initially leaked information to the *Guardian* (newspaper) in the Spring of 2013, and then to other media. *Snowden's* revelations were astonishing!

He claimed an unprecedented scope of surveillance by the U.S. government of both its citizens and our allies.

Snowden's explanation for his actions is revealed in the following quote: "I don't want to live in a society that does these sort of things [surveillance on its citizens]... I do not want to live in a world where everything I do and say is recorded."

Many people regard *Snowden* as a "whistleblower" and a "hero," others view him as a traitor. *Snowden* has defenders and critics on both sides of the aisle and among conservatives and liberals. In an August 9, 2013 News Conference *President Obama* commented about Mr. *Snowden* and seemed to take a modified position.

Spying on Ourselves

The President said: "We must earn the trust of the people." and "We can and must be more transparent." and finally, "America is not interested in spying on 'ordinary people.'" He didn't define who ordinary people are.

Under the guise (or justification) of detecting and preventing terrorism the country has engaged in a massive, unprecedented curtailment of freedoms and personal privacy. What do you think? Is it warranted, or would you prefer more constrained and targeted programs? Although the president (a former Constitutional Law professor) indicated he still thought *Snowden* violated the law and he felt the government's programs are not abusing (are compliant with) the law, the controversy accelerated a necessary review of the extent of government surveillance.

When the President of our country can emphatically state on national television (*Obama* on *Jay Leno's* Late Night Show): "There is no spying on Americans." And insist "We don't have a domestic spying program," and be proven a prevaricator three weeks later, he's got big credibility issues.

The ensuing revelation that the *National Security Agency* intercepted at least 56,000 emails a year from Americans who weren't suspected of having ties to terrorism was a major blow to our Fourth Amendment Rights. Since then we've also learned the Government is monitoring social media networks, internet browsing, and *GPS* locations.

The *Homeland Security Analyst Handbook* lists an extensive array of key words, including - and here's just a few:

> Airport, attack exercise, law enforcement, authorities, pork, shots, death, hostage, pipe bomb, agent, task force, Red Cross, Coast Guard, cops, authorities, detention, deaths, response, incident, facility, team, mitigation, police, hostage, riot, explosion, security, gangs, cloud, plume, toxic, chemical, infection, powder, gas, burn, virus, sick, swine, flu, tuberculosis, Public Health, exposure, collapse, power, smart, power lines, power, gunfight, Tijuana, Yuma, Tucson, border, drug, narcotics, violence, San Diego, Mexico, Columbia, El Paso, heroin, consular, strain vaccine, Tamiflu, epidemic, subway, bridge, dock, port, cancelled, BART, AMTRAK, infrastructure.

These words can draw unwanted Government attention to your internet communications. But should they? Think about it.

Let's say you decide to write an email, or make a post on *Facebook*, about your vacation and you write: "We left the airport on our way to San Diego. While there the Coast Guard team had a response to a boat explosion at one of the docks in the port. In the afternoon we crossed the border into Tijuana, where the agent asked about drugs. We were afraid of gangs, violence or getting sick in Mexico, so we thought it would be smart to return early to our hotel across the bridge in San Diego.

A very suspicious communication, wouldn't you say? Of course not, but it registers high in density of keywords on the Government's list!

And it could possibly make you a target of unwarranted and unwanted government suspicion and scrutiny.

When you see *China* referring to the *U.S.* as the world's biggest enemy of human rights you know we're in trouble. It's like everything the government does is either too much or too little, never "just right." If we meddle in foreign affairs we cause chaos, meddle with housing results in a crash, fool around with the economy it ends in recession, etc, etc. And our government spies never seem to rest, always vigilant and concerned that some damn American might be trying to exercise their "freedom of speech."

A Militarized Society

The war on terrorism combined with the war on drugs has also spawned a militarization of local police forces. Many have become more para-military with all the gear and equipment and specialized training. It's almost like we're living with an occupying force designed to keep us in line. Are you uncomfortable with this, or is it the price we pay to deter terrorism?

An eerie reminder of the dangers of our current situation came over half-a-century ago. On January 17, 1961 President (and 5 Star General) *Dwight D. Eisenhower* in his Presidential Farewell Address emphatically warned the nation of the dangers of the "Military-Industrial Complex."

Essentially his concern was that the military and industry would each, and jointly, pressure the government to spend more on the machinery of war. The military to expand their capabilities and might; industry to obtain lucrative defense contracts.

This prescient warning rings as true today as it did then. In fact the triggering event of 9/11 spurred an increase in military and security expenditures of 137% in the ten years following that horrific event.

[132]

OUT TO GET YOU

We're now spending more on national defense, the military and homeland security than any time since *World War II*.

Eisenhower always believed that the nation's security was closely
connected with our economic strength. He didn't think we could afford it then, and we sure as heck can't afford it now.

CNBC released an interesting report on the extent of Government contracts. The report issued in mid-2012 cited over one-half trillion
dollars in government contracts for F/Y 2011. As expected the biggest
recipients of this public largess were defense contractors.

Here, in order of largest total government contact amounts awarded to
these corporations:

1. *Lockheed Martin*
2. *Boeing*
3. *General Dynamics*
4. *Raytheon*
5. *United Technologies*
6. *SAIC (Science Applications International Corp.)*
7. *L-3 (LLL) Communications*
8. *BAE Systems*

The corporations on this list provide the government with everything
from military aircraft to surveillance technology and equipment. Sat-
ellites, helicopters, submarines and destroyers, vehicles, etc, are also
favorites on the government's shopping list. *Oshkosh Corporation*
(no. 9) has been a defense contractor for over 80 years! Think of the
consequences of this military-government-political relationship; the
lobbying the influence-peddling, etc.

More importantly how committed to world peace can these corporations be when a substantial portion or majority of their income comes
as a result of conflict, war, and international instability.

It should be noted that several of these contractors are also doing business with our international adversaries. A peaceful world is not a lucrative one for the defense industry.

It makes me sadly suspicious that the constant conflicts, military actions, terrorist threats, etc. are somehow tied to the profit motive and a cozy unhealthy relationship between a giant defense industry and a complicit, enabling government.

The defense industry since 9/11 has also morphed and expanded into the defense-homeland security-anti-terrorism industry. A genuine elephant in the room.

The Foreign Policy Trick

Although we can't seem to straighten out the mess at home, the U.S. government continues to delight in meddling in foreign affairs.

Our country spends approximately one-half of total world military expenditures although we only account for about six percent of the world's population.

Talk about military might! So if we're unsuccessful in persuading other nations to our way of thinking, we always have the subtle threat of overwhelming force.

The Constitution has several passages dealing with foreign affairs powers. The President is given authority to make treaties, and the Senate is given the authority to advise and consent (Article II, Section 2). The President is designated *Commander-in-Chief* of the Army and Navy (Article II, Section 2); but Congress was given authority to raise and support armies, and to provide and maintain a Navy (Article 1, Section 8, Clauses 12 and 13).

Congress alone has the power to declare war. The Congress is also given authority to define offenses against the law of nations and to set punishments for them (Article I, Section 8, Clause 10). Recent presidents have circumvented these requirements by trickery. E.g. substituting manipulative wording and ambiguous or euphemistic terminology -- it's not a war but a "conflict," or "military action," "offense," or a "police action."

Recent International Issues

Many of our recent misadventures in the volatile *Middle East* have had painful consequences like those in *Iraq* and *Afghanistan, Egypt, Tunisia* and *Libya*. But we continue to muddle and meddle. Now it's *Syria*. You can see another disaster coming.

While we curtail the freedoms of our people at home we advocate for expanded freedoms and democracy abroad. Is that hypocritical, or what? We love to tell other countries how they should run theirs. Does this make sense? Should we be orchestrating or assisting revolts in other nations? As *Russian* President *Vladimir Putin* commented in a *New York Times* opinion letter (9/11/13): "…the world increasingly sees America not as a model of democracy but as relying solely on brute force, cobbling coalitions together under the slogan "you're either with us or against us." *Putin* even took the opportunity to remind the American public and our leaders: "We are all different, but when we ask for the Lord's blessings, we must not forget that God created us equal." Strange words from the leader of a country not known for its concern for human rights, (and with wording strikingly similar to our own *Declaration of Independence*).

We might do well to exercise more caution and restraint in international affairs, and be less willing to throw our military weight and words of intimidation around.

The *United Nations*, as impotent as it often appears should be strengthened by its use as a conflict resolution agent, except of course, in cases of matters of imminent threat or national defense.

Our constant meddling in other nation's internal affairs has frequently turned allies into adversaries. In almost all cases resulted in resentment and confusion. Our support of leadership in other countries can "turn-on-a-dime" leaving foreign leaders bewildered and confused. Our meddling is also increasingly viewed as hypocritical.

While our expressed values support independence and freedom our policies and practices may not. Is it possible that our meddling is motivated by the political-military-industrial factions? For example, while we're advocating freedom and human rights we're actively suppressing them in our own country. The insidious and ever-expanding limitations resulting as a consequence of the *Patriot Act* being the most notable example.

Consequences of Foreign Entanglements and Nation Building or Destroying

Would we like it if other countries tried to do to us what we do to them? We abandon leaders who have supported us for years like *Mubarak* or *Kaddafi*, or to go back a little further- the *Shah* of *Iran*. We support their overthrow and what do we end up with?

Even worse and more unpredictable conditions. Worse leadership, bigger problems and hatred directed towards America. Just when you think it couldn't get any more horrible it does. When *George Bush* rallied our allies to intervene in *Iraq* because of the stockpiles of WMD's (weapons of mass destruction) what did we find? Nothing. What did we end up accomplishing?

Sure we deposed a brutal dictator but we destroyed a country, killed our young soldiers and *Iraqi* civilians in the process, and wasted hundreds of billions too.

[136]

Actual amounts are difficult to verify although *reuters.com* reports that the cost of the *Iraqi* war was in excess of $2 trillion! And if we include interest costs on the debt used to finance this war over the next four decades the total balloons to over $6T.

If we add in *Afghanistan* and *Pakistan* it becomes a real nightmare with another $1.7 trillion and again, amortized over the future, even more mind-boggling. And the most tragic aspect: There were 272,000 to 329,000 lives lost in the process. Of these over 4,000 were American soldiers, plus over 32,000 injured.

It goes on. In *Iraq* we spent another $272 billion in reconstruction that was mostly lost to private security firms, fraud and waste. And we continue to this day to pour money (that we don't have) and precious lives into the *Middle-East* sieve.

Politics of Intervention

Our "policies" concerning intervention into another country's affairs have a broad range: From expressions of concern to declaration of war. We have never been a nation known to shy away from conflict. However, our involvement has been uneven and unpredictable to the casual observer. In recent times we have expressed outrage at foreign government atrocities like *Saddam Hussein*'s attacks on the *Kurdish* minority in *Iraq* or *Assad*'s use of chemical agents against his own people in *Syria*.

If massacres occur (*Eastern*) *Europe* or the *Middle East* we're far more likely to intervene militarily than if similar offenses happen in *Asia*, and we're highly unlikely to engage when violations occur in *Africa* where genocides are more common e.g. *Sudan, Rwanda, Uganda, Congo*. It isn't that some lives are worth more than others it's that our decisions are political and financial. Some "crimes against humanity" are politically worthy of addressing and others not.

Our politicians look for support from their constituents, but military-involvement decisions are primarily made based on strategic value or risk. This may not be fair or appropriate, or consistent with our humanitarian values, but it's a reality.

Perhaps it's time to re-examine our foreign intervention policies because they're inconsistent, frequently ineffective, and we can't afford to run the world!

Foreign Service

Our Ambassadors to many nations are inept or inexperienced. Instead of selecting the most qualified candidates there is a long-standing practice of presidents nominating friends, donors and supporters to be the "face of America" on foreign soil.

All recent presidents have followed this model. In the first seven months of 2013 there were a total of 41 ambassadors selected, of those 23 (56%) had little or no diplomatic experience according to the *American Foreign Service Association*. For example, under *President Obama* major contributors to his campaign filled desirable ambassadorship posts in *Spain*, *Australia*, the *Dominican Republic* and *Singapore*. Five hundred thousand dollars or more might buy a plum assignment. What a way to run a country.

Of course the most sensitive, volatile and strategic assignments are generally filled with experienced, knowledgeable and capable career Foreign Service types. The politically-connected, moneyed supporters probably wouldn't want them anyway.

The Big Trick

The broad areas encompassing terrorism, defense, national security and foreign policy are obviously extremely important, sensitive, complicated, potentially dangerous and extraordinarily costly. They entail high-stakes, life and death decisions. These are number-one, top priority responsibilities that should be rationally managed and executed. However, they are rife with politicized decisions, awash in special interests, pander to certain factions, and often yield unforeseen outcomes. Trick is too mild a word to describe this.

America did not invent human rights. In a very real sense human rights invented America.

--Jimmy Carter

If we do everything right,
if we do it with absolute certainty,
there's still a 30% chance we're going to get it wrong.

– Vice President Joe Biden

Osama bin Laden is dead,
and General Motors is alive.

– Vice President Joe Biden

Though the people support the government;
the government should not support the people.

--Grover Cleveland

[140]

Chapter Fifteen

The Education Trick

A sinister trick at all levels, federal, state and local. The trick is to pretend to be supportive of education while undermining the quality, and increasing the costs. Essentially the government and politicians at all levels cater to the educational lobby. The teachers unions, the for-profit colleges, are powerful forces and voting blocks. The government seems only mildly interested in developing a world-class highly-educated workforce and preparing students for employment in the fields most in demand. They're more interested in votes.

I have been an educator for much of my life, primarily in higher education, teaching undergraduate and graduate courses at several top tier colleges and universities in *California*. When I moved to *Florida* I secured a position at a for-profit school, my first experience with a profit-based educational institution. But more about that later.

Public education is in trouble, particularly at the K-12 level. Grade inflation has resulted in many students earning better than perfect 4.0 GPA's. In fact an A+ overall record upon high school graduation is not uncommon. In most communities the schools are graded too. Grade inflation impacts this area as well, with most schools ranking above average. Students are also subjected to proficiency tests before they can be awarded a diploma.

With all this testing and ranking and high grades you would think that the educational system is performing at top levels. But is it? And are these graduates smarter and better prepared?

A majority of students are not ready for college, and entrance exam scores are falling. According to *ACT* only 39% of High School graduates in the class of 2013 were proficient in at least three of the four (English, Reading, Math, and Science) college readiness benchmarks, and only 24% were proficient in all four areas. The racial disparities were particularly disturbing with 43% of *Asians* qualifying in all areas but only 5% of *African-Americans*.

Michael Cohen, president of *Achieve*, a *Washington*-based nonprofit educational organization instrumental in the "Common Core State Standards," says the country continues to graduate large numbers of students who lack the academic skills to succeed in postsecondary education and training programs. "It's been the same news for a long time. We aren't moving the needle," he said.

Smarter or Dumber?

The lack of readiness to perform college-level academic work represents an astounding change and is at odds with the finding that average IQ's continue to rise. (Probably because the tests are written in an academic fashion and the test-takers have a more lengthy experience in academia.) In 1900 the average American had less than four years formal education, by 1950 twelve percent of Americans had a college education and today over fifty percent have gone to college.

A *British* study reported on the short-term memory loss associated with information technology. It seems that the younger generation has delegated so much of their memory tasks to *Google* and cellphones that they have retention difficulties.

[142]

The researchers have labeled this problem "cyber-dementia" and unlike the decreases in mental facility associated with aging this syndrome is appearing in teenagers and young adults. Think about yourself. Do you have difficulty remembering phone numbers, names and addresses? How about other types of data? I suspect we all do. Where this will all lead is debatable, although concerning.

The Government's "Contribution" to Education

Where does the government come in? Well, the educational system is a mess. The government increasingly relies on benchmarks, standards and ranking to define the quality of education. They don't devote much attention to the process, nor do they exert their considerable influence to match societal and workforce needs with curricula. And, they continue to provide loans to students attending programs of questionable value, oftentimes at inferior for-profit institutions of "learning." Is their goal to provide "welfare" to corporations offering marginal programs, to produce graduates with mismatched skills for employment demands, and/or to impoverish future generations? Perhaps it's all of these, but more likely they don't have a clue or an interest. Besides, big-money lobbyists and campaign contributors come from the ranks of the mega for-profit educational corporations.

There's also a huge mismatch between education and business. Because students often choose fields they "like" rather than fields that offer the best career opportunities you hear many graduates complaining they can't find a job or they're underemployed. It seems that it would be in the educators' best interest, the students' best interest, and the nation's best interest to provide full-disclosure.

Perhaps to offer data about "hot" fields, best career opportunities and job prospects beginning in high school and certainly at college entrance. An informed student can then decide what's best for them.

I'm not talking about steering students into specific fields, just providing them with information. The notion that everyone should have a college education is just plain wrong.

And it's a costly, discouraging, frustrating model. As I mentioned, I speak from experience. I have encountered students barely able to read and write expecting to get A's and B's. Why were these students encouraged to enroll in college in the first place? And why were they admitted? The sad fact is colleges want their money and their bodies. They need students in the seats and benefit from enrollment growth.

Education for Making a Living

Most students know the acronym "STEM" (Science, Technology, Engineering and Mathematics) because these are fields in demand. The country needs students- and teachers -in these areas and grads will find plenty of opportunities.

Every career doesn't require a college education, and many of the highest paying fields are in the trades. Refrigeration mechanics, automotive mechanics, air-conditioning technicians, electricians, com-computer repair, general contactors, etc.

There are also numerous specialized jobs in various other areas. Many of these jobs offer opportunities to "go into business" as an entrepreneur.

The point of this discussion is that not everyone needs a college education, although the government's policies seem to indicate they think they do. Every citizen needs a sufficient education to earn a living and understand the basics of commerce. Beyond that an understanding of the republic in which they live and the functions and responsibility of the democratic process.

Making Money Off Students

I mentioned earlier that I taught at a for-profit college in *Florida*. What I saw there was a disconnect between the student's needs and institutional responsibility. The school would sign up students for a two-year degree program costing over $30,000. Many of these students had no business in college. They were largely unprepared and often marginally fluent in the English language. Most were *Caribbean* immigrants (primarily *Haitian* or *Cuban*) and *English* was their second language. The demands for profitability and shareholder value regularly took precedence over the students' best interests. They received a marginal education, a huge financial obligation, and a degree from a second-rate institution accredited by an inferior accrediting agency. All in the name of $$$$$. The incentive was government student loan money.

Guaranteed income resulting in high profitability for the corporation. I'm still ashamed of my participation in this segment of the education industry, and the government should be ashamed of their sponsorship.

College Costs are Out of Control

As mentioned above, college is now extremely expensive. In fact, so expensive that most students (and families) are priced out of the system. I remember my tuition at the *University of Washington* a ("Land Grant") public institution. It's easy to remember because it never changed while I was in attendance. The $100 per Quarter tuition was fixed by the State legislature and remained in place for many years.

Today's students don't have it so easy. To meet its agenda of degrees for everyone and "affordable education," the Government stepped in with student loans. These loans can easily total more than a modest home costs in many areas. And, just as with the housing bubble the government has created a huge education bubble. The $850+ billion dollars in Government backed student loans is so huge it now exceeds total U.S. credit card debt.

Just as with the housing market, government intervention has resulted in an inflationary spiral of costs. You would think they would learn from the trick they played by convincing Americans that everyone should own a home. But they are playing the same trick on families again. This time it involves convincing them that all children should go to college. Every family should not buy a house, and every young person does not belong in college.   And just like homeowners became buried in mortgage debt underwritten by government agencies, students are now buried in easily obtained government underwritten debt when they graduate from college. And colleges continue to expand, raise salaries, fund new building projects, and further increase tuition in an artificially created spiral as a consequence of the government's irresponsible policies.   As a cynical twist government regulations do not allow discharging student debts even when borrowers file for bankruptcy. This is permanent debt.

Public Schools

The government has not improved public K-12 education. That process is best left to the States and local communities. A controversial book by *Charlotte Thomson Iserbyt* (a Senior Education Policy Advisor during the *Reagan* Administration) is titled "The Deliberate Dumbing Down of America."

The author makes the case that the *Department of Education* has been modifying public school requirements to further a social agenda and not concentrating on preparing students for future careers and advanced education.

Now they want to "fix" higher education. Our public higher education; Colleges and Universities are still the best in the world. Leave them alone!

At the *University of New York at Buffalo* on August 22, 2013 *President Obama* touted a new "grading plan" for colleges. Remember what we did with K-12 schools? (How's that working for you?) Well, now the Feds would like to impose various measurement systems in higher education. Under the goal of "Educational Affordability" various benchmarks and outcomes would be imposed. I don't consider the Government an expert in cost-effectiveness and cost-containment. Kind of like asking your bankrupt, spendthrift uncle for tips on how to balance your budget. (Even better if his name is "Sam.")

Educator Salaries

Teaching no longer has "bottom of the heap" payscales. I'm pro education but I think in most cases teachers are fairly compensated. Yes, it's a tough job, although a rewarding one. Starting salaries for teachers (nationwide average) are only $35,672 (*nea.org*). However, pay usually increases fairly rapidly.

The average tenured teacher in *California* earns $67,871; in *Massachusetts* $70,752; and in New York $72,708. (Just don't teach in *S. Dakota* where it's only $39,850.)   Public University instructors do much better of course with a full-professors at *UCLA* making an average of $167,000; *U of Michigan* $158,900; and *U of Texas* at $143,200. Although they trail behind big private schools like the *University of Chicago* at $203,600 and at *Columbia University,* $212,300.

Increased K-12 educator salaries haven't translated into superior education or improved student performance.   A *Cato Institute* study charted education spending vs *NEAP* (National Assessment of Educational Progress) reading and math test scores from 1970 through 2003 on the same graph.   The chart had to be extended vertically to allow for an accurate representation of costs.   Not so for student performance. In fact test results increased insignificantly in math and actually declined in reading.   The results were oddly flat with little movement in either direction overall. The disturbing conclusion was that "higher public school spending slows the economy." While I believe that interpretation might not be warranted by the facts, I do believe the input in terms of money has not yielded an equivalent increase in terms of student performance results.   If one would look at productivity in other segments of our economy they would see phenomenal increases in private sector productivity and cost-effectiveness.   Public education is clearly a laggard.

If we believe the key to higher performance is to keep throwing more money at education in the hopes of improving the process that approach is clearly flawed. I believe most *Catholic* schools are superior to public schools and they're much lower-cost operations.

International Education Comparisons

Each year the *OECD* (*Organization for Economic Cooperation and Development*) produces an "Education at a Glance" report comparing member nations on various indicators.

[148]

(This information is from the 2012 issue.) The member nations include the most developed countries of the world. In these countries the percentage of adults with the "equivalent of a college degree" rose to 30%. In the U.S. it's over 40%. Although for readers who believe we're at the top—you're incorrect. That honor goes to our northern neighbor, *Canada*; the only nation in the world with over 50%.

We rank number four, behind *Canada, Israel* and *Japan*. The remainder of the top ten, in order, are: *New Zealand, South Korea, United Kingdom, Finland, Australia*, and *Ireland*. There is a correlation with *GDP* per capita supporting the notion that education is positively correlated with personal incomes. However, there are some notable exceptions such as: *South Korea* and *Israel*. Those countries have disproportionately lower *GDP* per capita despite having extremely educated populations.

We Don't Want to See Headlines Like This:

US adults are dumber than the average human
By Associated Press
October 8, 2013 | 10:45am

WASHINGTON — It's long been known that America's school kids haven't measured well compared with international peers. Now, there's a new twist: Adults don't either.
In math, reading and problem-solving using technology – all skills considered critical for global competitiveness and economic strength – American adults scored below the international average on a global test, according to results released Tuesday.   -
Japan, Finland, Canada, Netherlands, Australia, Sweden, Norway, Flanders-Belgium, Czech Republic, Slovak Republic, and Korea all scored significantly higher than the United States in all three areas on the test.
(excerpts from A.P. story printed in *N.Y. Post*)

Despite the comparatively high levels of schooling, Americans don't fare well on standardized tests, indicating that it isn't the number of years spent in the educational system that counts, but the quality of learning and instruction that took place.

High Cost / Low Quality?

In education as with healthcare, Americans pay the most. It seems as though we pay more in every area where the Government has a heavy presence. In fact per student expenditures are around 50% more than our peers. The 15%+ of GDP that we spend (on all levels of education) is, as an extreme example, over twice the 6.5% that *Israel* spends. Although we spend the most we don't get the most.

Our secondary school dropout rate is significantly higher; our college completion rate is lower. And although college grads have traditionally had lower rates of unemployment, at this time over 50% of <u>recent college grads</u> are either unemployed or underemployed.

Another misconception concerns educational funding. Perhaps counter-intuitively countries having higher levels of education also have among the highest amounts of <u>private</u> sources of education support, including tuition and donations. (In the U.S. its 28%; in *South Korea* >40%.)

Don't Blame the Teachers

I want to be clear that I'm not blaming our teachers. They do the best job they can under the circumstances. The educational dilemma is very complex and encompasses societal problems, family issues, and cultural matters. Most importantly, however, blame the government. The educational system has been politicized and is governed by misguided objectives which translate into counter-productive strategies.

[150]

Educational curricula, values, policies, textbooks and procedures shouldn't be the prerogative of politicians and bureaucrats. Parents and teachers want and know what's best for their children. The educational-government complex interferes, subverts, and weakens the process of knowledge transfer, academic curiosity, and most of all, performance.

Education and Government Literacy

It's no joke that Americans know very little about their government. A *Newsweek* (March, 2011) poll of 1,000 American citizens revealed an astonishing level of ignorance. The poll required participants to take the Citizenship test offered to those applying to become *Naturalized Citizens*. Based on survey results a staggering number could not qualify to be citizens of their own country. Thirty-eight percent failed!

A sampling of survey results include: 29% couldn't name the Vice President; 73% didn't know why we fought the "Cold War;" 67% didn't realize we have a capitalist economic system, 44% didn't know what the *Bill of Rights* is; 6% didn't even know the calendar date of *Independence Day*. This lack of knowledge can be attributed to poor education, but more importantly to lack of interest.

Europeans are much savvier about politics and world events than Americans. They have much more of a world view, and typically receive a sounder education. And, most importantly they have an *interest* in the world around them.

Become informed! Since you can't count on government-run schools to educate you (or your children) about government you need to take responsibility for educating yourself.

An appreciation for the importance of a knowledgeable electorate is the first step. Make sure you're included in that category.

Just for fun you can try and pass a sample Citizenship test on-line at http://www.uscis.gov/portal/site/uscis. I suspect the readers of this book, because of your interest in the topic will fare much better than the typical test-taker. And I think you'll be surprised at how easy it really is.

Bottom Line

You can't trust the government to make sure you or your offspring have a decent education. And because they have tricked you into be-lieving college is essential, while at the same time making sure it's unaffordable they have made it a "no win" situation. Combined with a devastated economy increasingly service-sector dominated, a dearth of professional positions and an abundance of minimum wage jobs, the future for many college grads doesn't look that bright. In spite of all of this a college degree is still a "passport" to professionalism and economic security. It isn't for everyone but for intelligent, disciplined and motivated students it can be a real game-changer.

Chapter Sixteen

Our Politicians

Now we get to talk about the "tricksters"; the government's 'Magister Ludi' pulling the strings of power in Washington, D.C., State Capitols, Counties and Cities throughout the nation. However, the trick is on them too! Because they owe their power to the really powerful: the Parties, the corporate giants, the Lobbyists, and the Contributors and "payback is a bitch."

They're certainly a bunch of characters! We are often amused by the antics of our politicians although most of their shenanigans are not funny!

A Politician Named Weiner

The first name which comes to mind when thinking about contemporary politicians is – *Weiner*! Yes *Anthony Weiner*, the sex-addicted internet exhibitionist, former Congressional Representative, and 2013 *New York* Mayoral candidate who doesn't have a clue. *Weiner* has brought fun back into politics. I could hardly wait to see the latest headlines in the *New York Post*, or the *Daily News*. It provided me with comic relief from those ridiculous all-too-serious politicians who want us to believe they're normal. Everyone knows politicians are performers, and the political arena is a circus.

[153]

But back to *Weiner*. With a name like his you'd think he'd be a little more careful, but it's all part of the fun. Let me remind you of some of the headlines. Here we go: "Tip of the Weiner," "Weiner Probe," "Obama Beats Weiner," "Weiner Pulls Out," "Mounting Pressure on Weiner," "Weinergate," "Tough Package to Handle." "Weiner Hard to Swallow," and "Weiner Gets Grilled."

Think you're done; not yet! Here are some more puns: "Hide the Weiner," "Weiner is Shrinking," "For a Good Time Elect Weiner," "Weiner Roasted," "Weiner Exposed," "Weiner Finally Yanks Himself," "Too Hard to Stop," "Beat It!," "Stick a Fork in Weiner!," "Weiner's Second Coming," "Cuomo Spanks Weiner," "Dirty Weiner Plunges in the Hole!," "Weiner's Rise and Fall," "Couldn't Keep it Up!" "Weiner goes Soft!" "Weiner Thrusts into Campaign!" "Weiner keeps Going!" "Weiner Makes it Hard" and, "Can Weiner Keep it Up?"

And then, after being "exposed" when he tried to cover his tracks, while continuing his Internet antics, he used an alias. The pseudonym he picked: *"Carlos Danger."* Hilarious. Too funny!

Needless to say the infamous Mr. *Weiner* lost his bid for the Mayor of *New York* in the September Primary. He won only about 5% of the vote on election day.

Weiner "Wanabe's"

We may laugh at *Weiner*'s escapades, but these types of scandals have swirled around politicians throughout our history. Here are a few of the politicians recently caught in scandals ranging from tickling staffers to sex with prostitutes, to gay affairs, extramarital adventures, fathering children out of wedlock, exhibitionism, sexual harassment, etc: *Herman Cain* (R-Pres. Candidate), *John Edwards*, (R- N.C., Pres. Candidate), and Gov. *Arnold Schwarzenegger* (R-Ca.),

[154]

Also, Rep. *Mark Souder* (R-Ind.), Rep. *Eric Massa* (R-N.Y.), Rep. *Vito Fosella* (D-N.Y.*)*, *Larry Craig* (R-Idaho), and Rep. *Tim Mahoney* (D-Fl.), Rep. *Chip Pickering* (R-Miss.), Gov. *James McGreevy* (D-N.J.), Sen. *David Vitter* (R-La.), Rep. *Mark Foley* (R-Fla.), Gov. *Mark Sanford* (R-S.Car.), Sen. (candidate) *Jack Ryan* (R-Il.).

The above-named politicos are only the most recent offenders, and are only those who became ensnared in sex-related scandals.

Corruption

Personally, I don't care about who our politicians sleep with. Of course it speaks to character, particularly when it involves reckless behavior, sexual harassment or coercion and so forth. What bothers me much more is when politicians use their position, power, and influence to unfair or illegal advantage.

In fraud, corruption and waste your politicians certainly "lead by example!" Especially when they receive kickbacks, reward supporters and contributors with government contracts, or engage in behaviors which subvert or compromise the best interests of their constituents and/or the country.

I don't like it when our politician employees take excessive trips at public expense, pad their expense accounts, sponsor special-interest but counter-productive legislation, or use their position to impede legislation in the public interest.

Or when they fail to honor the wishes and best interests of those who elected them, intentionally deceive or mislead the public, compromise public safety or national security or engage in any number of unethical, dishonest or illegal acts.

[155]

Congressional Demographics

Do your Congressional representatives resemble you? Certainly-- if you're a rich White male Protestant Attorney.

Congressional demographics are often reviewed and regularly reported on. The electorate wants to know who's representing our interests.

Who are our legislators? Can our Representatives and Senators relate to us and our problems? Are they average Americans who got a lucky break? One clue is: Congress is often referred to as a millionaire's club.

They're predominately older (average age of Representatives is 57, and Senators 62), white *and* male (67%), wealthy (average $7M net worth for Reps, $14M for Senators), educated (93% with at least a Bachelor's degree), been around for a while (average tenure 9.1 years in the House, 10.2 years in the Senate).

Being a member of the Congressional "Millionaires Club" certainly has its benefits. A great salary, wonderful benefits, first-class healthcare, access to information and people who can make you even wealthier, boondoggle trips to far-flung exotic locales, etc.

Big Money for Lawmakers and other Public Officials

Salaries and other compensation for members of Congress have increased throughout history. In the 1800's Congressmen earned $6 a day. In the 1950's they were making $22,500 annually and currently their salary is $174,000. The *Speaker of the House* makes $233,000, and the Majority and Minority Leaders $193,400 each.

But this isn't the whole story. Members of Congress also receive an array of other allowances including Health and Life insurance, mailing allowances, travel expenses. Additionally there are Administrative and Staff allowances, Legislative staff assistance, along with other enumerated categories; ranging in total from over $2 million to $3 and three-quarters million. And a number of miscellaneous perks.

In effect, each Congressional office is a multi-million dollar business. However, the big money is not from salaries, benefits, travel, offices and staff, it's from investments. Congressmen are limited to 15% extra income derived from outside work, their profession or other earnings. There is no such limit on investment proceeds. While investors are typically barred from using "insider information" to make profitable or strategic trades, Congress is all about "inside information." Think about it. If you were regularly meeting with the *Chairman of the Federal Reserve*, the *Secretary of the Treasury*, Business Leaders and Billionaires you might become a more astute investor too.

Let's make this clear, I don't begrudge any of these office holders their salaries, and I think the President's $400 thousand is a bargain. I don't think any of their compensation is outrageous.

Generous but not excessive, particularly when we read about million dollar salaries for officials in a small town (*Bell*) in California. Or *Miami*, where I live, where 3 Mayors, (of *Miami Lakes, Sweetwater, and Homestead*), weren't satisfied with their paychecks and were arrested during the summer of 2013 for kickbacks, bribes, and unlawful compensation. These types of criminal or unethical behaviors are actually quite common across the country; so common that most voters aren't surprised in the least.

To Serve the Country?

Congress is elected to do the country's business. To make laws. To make the country better. But "Laws are like sausages, its better not to see them being made." (*Otto von Bismarck*) Laws are made by compromise and concession, favors and tradeoffs, alliances and deals. This is why it's so messy.

Legislators don't necessarily vote for good legislation, they vote for legislation they, or their party, can benefit from in some fashion. In order to make a deal "riders" are often attached to legislative bills that have little or nothing to do with the bill. Usually these riders involve special interests influencing a particular legislator to attach the rider to gain that (special interest) person or group's support. Other riders are created to impress the voters in the officeholder's district or to bring federal money or jobs: like funding a road, a bridge, building or special project. Occasionally its scope can be extremely narrow and specific such as legalizing an immigrant or group. These are deplorable, although common practices. Influential members of Congress might even include a "poison pill" provision to make it unlikely it will be signed into law. These types of tricks make for poor legislation. In some cases, downright lousy laws.

Another issue impacting our elected leaders and their ability to govern is that running for office is now a full-time, perpetual job.

The amounts of money required and the necessity for constant media attention has caused this. Years ago I don't recall political fundraisers throughout the officeholder's term. As it got closer to elections yes, but not always. Now the candidates are always running for office, and even when they are faced with term-limits they're running to raise money for their party and their presumed replacement. This is more than unfortunate. It distracts our leaders, the public, and the government from their primary purpose—governance.

Politics has become a game of big money, not big ideas.

As I mentioned earlier in the book, I'm an independent thinker and voter. I really don't trust hardly any of them. I certainly believe it is the utmost folly to vote a straight party ticket. And, I believe in supporting and contributing to individual candidates, not parties.

Contemporary Definition of "Politician"

Just for fun, let's see how those who contribute to the *Urban Dictionary* (primarily "Gen Y" and "Millennials") define the word Politician. Here are the top two:

1. A person who practices politics.
   "Politics" is derived from the words "poly" meaning "many", and "tics" meaning "blood-sucking parasites."
   a) One who was perfected the art of lying.
   b) A highly paid yes-man.
2. People that should never, ever be trusted under any circumstances.

Politicians have traditionally ranked low on measures of ethics, trust, admiration and respect. In the *Gallup* Survey on "Professional Honesty and Ethics" conducted Nov. 26-29, 2012, members of Congress were ranked next to the bottom – with only car salesmen ranking lower. Nurses were ranked highest.

[159]

Fun Info

At the height of the Congressional impasse on the budget and debt
ceiling pollsters revealed that Americans ranked Congress below
root canals, colonoscopies, traffic jams, Genghis Kahn, and cock-
roaches. (www.publicpolicypolling.com).

In *Canada* medical professionals and firefighters rank at the top of
"trusted professionals" and politicians are again at the bottom with
only telemarketers, car salesmen and psychics ranked lower. (*Readers
Digest* [Canada] May, 2012).

Why Should They Care About You?

We've already established that our "leaders" are quite different from
the average American. Let me count the ways... They're RICH. You
may not be. They have a high income. You might not. They have a
prestigious job. You may just "work for a living." They work in what
could be considered a "Palace." Your working environment might not
be as elaborate. They have an excellent healthcare plan and coverage.
Many Americans don't. They have lots of breaks and vacations. You
might just get one to four weeks. They party and schmooze a lot. You
probably don't have time for that. They meet with dignitaries and
business leaders, perhaps even celebrities. Most of us don't move in
those circles. People are often offering them "contributions" and support. If people offered you these "gifts" you'd probably worry about
their sanity or you going to jail. And despite all of this they are considered con men (and women), despised by many and considered
unethical and untrustworthy. It's quite a conflict. And, unfortunately
you don't make much of a difference to them. They know who does,
however. The big supporters, the ones with money and clout, whether
individuals or organizations, and they cater to them.

[160]

If someone with "influence" or "connections" needs access to a politician they'll get it. Some "average" citizens do manage to get on their "radar" (either in a positive or negative way) by making themselves "visible." They write to their elected officials, attend speeches and fundraisers, participate in campaigns, or send emails.

Perhaps you should go and visit with your elected Senator or Representative in your State Capitol, or even *Washington D.C.* Or you may want to observe them in their natural habitat from the Visitor's Gallery in the House or Senate.

I've done such things and highly recommend it. You'll probably feel overwhelmed and very patriotic. You might even get "goosebumps" at the majesty and history of the edifices. Either way you'll have to contact their office for availability and "passes."

They Work for You

A couple of times in this book I've reminded you that our Government "leaders" work for you. It may not seem like it, but the "public servants" work for you. Elected officials are your employees. It's easier to think in terms of a workplace analogy. And it's difficult to wrap your brain around the concept of multiple bosses. In some cases millions of bosses. It's like me trying to call *President Obama* or *Marco Rubio* (one of the U.S. Senators representing my State of *Florida*) into my office.

You can imagine: "Now look here *Barack*," (or *Marco*) you just haven't been a satisfactory employee." "You need to 'shape up' or I'll have to 'write you up,' maybe 'give you an 'Improvement Needed' evaluation." It isn't going to happen! But remember: it's supposed to be Government "of the people, by the people and for the people."

I'm a person (one OF the people) just like the candidates, who along with many other people decided to elect one of us (BY the people), to an office where they can do stuff FOR me (and for others like me).

Somehow the bond between the electorate and the elected has been severed or at least damaged. Most officials seem distant and arrogant. They're more interested in working for themselves and their friends than us. But we hired them and we pay them.

If you think of "outside income," or "supplemental income," worse yet "bribes" or "kickbacks," that could explain their lack of accountability and responsiveness to the people who elected them.

Besides, they believe that the people who really elected them are the major contributors and supporters who fund their campaigns and sponsor their ads. We're just the dupes (or dopes) who swayed in accordance with the real power brokers' money and wishes.

A Not So Peculiar Voting Strategy

In recent years I've adopted a voting strategy which you might not approve of. My basic philosophy is anti-incumbent.

When faced with a choice where I don't have strong feelings about either candidate, particularly in local (county and city) elections, I vote for the newcomer. I look at it this way: It takes a term or two for the elected official to become corrupt. So why not take a chance on the new candidate.

It takes time to learn how to steal efficiently, become completely beholden to special interests, and to develop political machinery that will almost guarantee re-election, so through my vote I want to disrupt and delay that process.

A final thought on the subject of our political leaders. They've changed. Instead of the idealists who formed the Country, or the pragmatists who helped guide us through the nineteenth and twentieth centuries, we've inherited the larcenous who want to fleece us to satisfy their own selfish goals.

Government's view of the economy could be summed
up in a few short phrases: If it moves, tax it.
If it keeps moving, regulate it.
And if it stops moving, subsidize it.

--Ronald Reagan

Nations, like individuals, are punished
for their transgressions.

--Ulysses S. Grant

Fear is the foundation of most governments.

--John Adams

You can fool some of the people all the time, and those
are the ones you want to concentrate on.

--George W. Bush

It is to be regretted that the rich and powerful too often
bend the acts of government to their own
selfish purposes.

--Andrew Jackson

Chapter Seventeen

A Culture of Corruption?

You probably know the places most famous for corruption, such as: Washington, D.C., Chicago, Detroit, and New York. The saying "power corrupts and absolute power corrupts absolutely" is applicable.

Who are the biggest crooks in the Country? The Mafia, Drug Cartels, jailbirds, welfare cheats, income tax evaders, petty criminals, marijuana growers, shoplifters? Is it corporations? Or the Financial and Banking community? The government?

Corruption at the State Level

In 2012 the *Center for Public Integrity* graded states on various corruption indices (333 metrics in 14 categories). The result of their study was a ranking by state on measures of corruption. According to their findings the most corrupt States are: *Georgia, South Dakota, Wyoming, Virginia, Maine, South Carolina, North Dakota*, and *Michigan*. Each of these states scored an overall grade of "F." But before you feel too smug about not living in one of these states, no State earned an 'A" and only five states achieved a "B+." Over half of the states earned a D+ or lower!

The researchers found the most corrupt states had "stagnant" politics with one political party (*Republican* or *Democrat*); states with a "machine" in place. "Machines want to protect themselves."

There are some big surprises among the least corrupt States: 1) *New Jersey*, 2) *Connecticut*, 3) *Washington*, 4) *California*, and, 5) *Nebraska*. But the very reason these scores are so high is frequently because their troubled past (particularly in New Jersey's case) resulted in enhanced public scrutiny, powerful watchdog agencies, and increased intolerance of corruption.

Private Sector Comparisons

For comparison with the non-government sector, here are the most corrupt (according to the *Daily Beast*) industries:

Utilities, Wall Street/Securities, Telecommunications, Construction, Media. Aren't you surprised Wall Street didn't come in #1? I was.

Now that we've looked at States and private sector industries, the broader question is how the United States stacks up against other governments and whether we're living up to our reputation as a bastion of freedom.

It's all a Matter of Perspective

How corrupt is the United States? You might ask "compared to what?" Well, compared with other countries. And, it just so happens that there is a "Corruption Perceptions Index" ranking 176 countries. Periodic studies sponsored by *Transparency International* utilizing data provided by organizations such as the *World Bank, the Economist, Freedom House, Global Insight,* and *World Justice Project*, are reported with nations ranked by levels of perceived corruption.

In the 2012 report *Denmark, Finland, New Zealand, Sweden, Singapore, Switzerland, Australia, Norway, Canada, Netherlands, Iceland and Luxembourg*, were ranked as the least corrupt countries. Next came *Germany, Hong Kong, Barbados, Belgium, Japan and the United Kingdom*. The *United States* ranked nineteenth, about on a par with *Chile* (ranked #20). This is still a very high ranking, but not as high as we deserve, or the American public expects. As the report's authors state: "...it's clear that corruption is a major threat facing humanity. Corruption destroys lives and communities, and undermines countries and institutions. It generates popular anger that threatens to further destabilise (sic) societies and exacerbate violent conflicts." Obviously if this is true we need to be watchful of our government at all levels and the private sector as well.

And two thirds of the countries examined have a serious corruption problem as indicated by a score of 50 or less. *Liberia* and *Mongolia* are at the bottom of the list.

"Corruption amounts to a dirty tax, and the poor and most vulnerable are its primary victims." So, how do we counter the effects of public sector corruption?

The report on corruption contains some sage advice: "The Governments need to integrate anti-corruption actions into all aspects of decision-making. They must prioritise (sic) better rules on lobbying and political financing, make public spending and contracting more transparent, and make public bodies more accountable."

Always remember, if your politicians, elected officials or government are mismanaging funds, misappropriating funds, padding or inflating costs or in any way being inept or dishonest—they're stealing from you! It's your government and your money!

Part of the Culture

This gets us back to the basic question: Do we have a "Culture of Corruption?" And the answer seems to be YES. Perhaps not as bad as during other periods in our history, but not as good as we've been either, and we deserve better.

It is endemic at all levels of government and in the private sector, and it's getting worse. More than three-quarters of Americans believe "political parties are the most corrupt, followed by the legislature, the media, public officials and businesses." Sixty percent of Americans say corruption is on the increase and only 10% feel it's getting better. (*U.S. News*, July 10, 2013).

Chapter Eighteen

Customer Service

Customer service is not characterized as a "trick" in this book be-cause nobody would fall for it. In many cases government offices and officials don't even pretend to offer quality customer service. If you have some time on your hands or need a hearty laugh read "Customer Service Standards for Federal Employees" in the gov.info.library. If you need a reminder of how bad service is at the local level visit a DMV Office in almost anywhere in the country.

Would you keep patronizing a company that offered high prices and low quality? Certainly not! But with the government you often have no choice. What are you going to do—go to another government? Government is notoriously inefficient. Perhaps not as bad as the *Bulgarian Bureaucracy* (I just like the sound of that) but nowhere near excellence. Typically they overcharge for their service, overpay their employees, provide inferior products, don't keep pace with the marketplace, are not competitive, and really don't care too much about how you feel about it.

You are the Customer

In addition to being their employer you are the government's customer. You're entitled to good service at reasonable cost. Without you, and millions like you, they couldn't stay in business.

[169]

However, here again they seem to act as though they're in charge. That we don't matter. And we've inadvertently contributed to that mindset and attitude through our own negligence and lack of feedback. It's a two-way street. If we expect more the government will, at some point, respond. (They're not noted for fast response times.) It's time for a new performance model and improved accountability. "Pay for Performance" is what it's called. Not pay for non-performance or poor performance. And how is their performance, anyway? We got a clue when government agencies were compared with their private sector counterparts. With few notable exceptions they didn't do well. And those who did well have products that we value more or trust more (Consular Offices, Weather Service).

How is Your Government Doing?

You have to give the government credit. At the Federal level they actually perform an assessment—it's called the *American Customer Satisfaction Index*. The results are predictable; the government always scores lowest of any economic sector.

Whether it's Hotels & Food, Finance & Insurance, Healthcare, Retail, Information or Transportation, they all score higher than your government.

[170]

Government's at the bottom, and a well-deserved distinction it is! There are some specific exceptions, however. The *SBA* (*Small Business Administration*), *Consular Services*, and the *National Weather Service* score rather highly and are comparable to the high scoring private sector companies. So it's evidently not impossible for the government to deliver quality service and have satisfied customers. Of all federal departments *Homeland Security* and *Treasury* score at the bottom although there are a couple of private firms that rank even lower. And, while overall performance is ranked low, customer service in handling complaints is worse. Even though on a percentage basis the government receives a small fraction (10%) of complaints when compared with their private sector counterparts. And only airlines do as poor a job in handling them.

The worst category for government isn't service. They're terrible at that, but respect for their performance and capabilities is even lower, with only 36% (in 2011) reporting overall confidence in the government. Specific agencies score much better but this is a real red flag. The results are similar to trust in Congress, the people who make our laws, and in whom the American people have almost no confidence. What a horrible irony.

A Recent Rollout Example

In October, 2013 we saw another example of the government's commitment to service excellence. You would think the Government would want to have a trouble-free rollout of a new public service or program but you don't understand the perversity of the political mind. Political motives *always* take precedence over efficiency, effectiveness, quality or customer service.

Throughout this book I have referred to the *Affordable Healthcare Act* as "*Obamacare*." I felt comfortable using this informal label because the President (*Obama*) regularly referred to his signature accomplishment by using the term.

[171]

(Incidentally, I'll bet the other presidents responsible for signing major social programs into law wish they would have thought to attach their names more directly to their programs. Then we might have *Roosevelt-security* instead of *Social Security* and *Johnson-care* instead of *Medicare*.)

When *Obamacare* finally rolled out on October 1st 2013 public and political aspirations were high. After all, the program had been under attack since its inception as a proposal, then a bill, then a program. The *Republican* led *House of Representatives* had unsuccessfully tried to delay it, defund it, kill it for years, but like a horror movie zombie it refused to die. With great anticipation the new $400-$600 million Federal website, *www.healthcare.gov,* or *www.obama-care.org* went live and millions of consumers, curious citizens, politicians and reporters tried to log on. They tried, and waited, then tried again. They got messages informing them the system was "down" or undergoing "scheduled maintenance." Almost nobody was able to fully access the site and complete their insurance signup through the government sponsored "marketplace." This continued for the first day, second day, second week, third and fourth weeks, etc. The *Republicans* were saying "see, we told you so! The *Canadian* firm *CGI had* designed it and was put on notice to fix it quick! *Consumer Reports* advised its readers to avoid the site "for at least another month."

The insurance companies were complaining about the lack of enrollees. The public was complaining about the excessive downtime and system unavailability. The Administration refused to provide enrollment data, so only insiders knew the extent of the problem. Congressmen demanded data, but the Administration balked saying it would be available eventually, maybe next month. Two weeks into the enrollment period newspapers were running headlines: "Obamacare enrollees become urban legend." Everybody had heard of them but nobody knew one. This was embarrassing. No, not really....the spin was: It was evidence of success and "overwhelming interest" in the program. Leave it to politicians to explain away failures and never take responsibility.

We Don't Complain Enough

Often citizens don't complain due to fear of retribution. We shouldn't have to live in fear of our government. Afraid they'll spy on us, audit us, put us on a no-fly list, label us as a security threat, terminate our *Social Security*, confiscate our weapons; drive us into destitution or insanity or oblivion. These are abusive tactics and reminiscent of the intimidation suffered by many immigrants who came here to avoid such practices.

Our government needs to become accountable to, and supportive of, the people. But if you, through your passivity, allow their abuses, poor service, and lack of respect, it will undoubtedly continue. You see, Government Approval ratings are a measure of their failure, not their success. If the government were a business it would be the oldest business in America. So if they had any intention to improve, it would have been done by now. Any other business that wished to remain in business would have made it their *business* to get better.

Yet the Government has expanded dramatically, grown exponentially in scope, size and cost but has this growth resulted in better service for the typical citizen? In a few respects the answer would have to be *certainly*. But in most respects no! We've always had a military to protect us, and a system to mete justice. We've always had a governance system in place. Unwanted, superfluous and unnecessary services don't count especially if they're poorly delivered.

If the government "gives" you *Social Security*, they're not actually "giving" you anything. You paid for it. Likewise with medical care, highways, postal service, police and fire protection and every other service or "benefit" you can think of. And they may be the most expensive and inefficient deliverer of these services.

I've mentioned this before, I'm not anti-government. But I am anti bloated, inefficient, unresponsive, arrogant, intrusive, vindictive, punitive, power and money-hungry, poor customer-service government. And I'm sure you are too.

[173]

If the people cannot trust their government to do the job for which it exists - to protect them and to promote their common welfare - all else is lost.

--Barack Obama

There is not a liberal America and a conservative America - there is the United States of America. There is not a Black America and a White America and Latino America and Asian America - there's the United States of America.

--Barack Obama

Americans... still believe in an America where anything's possible - they just don't think their leaders do.

--Barack Obama

Chapter Nineteen

How Much Government is Enough?

The trick here is to grow the government by portraying it as the only solution to the enormous problems confronting the nation. There are too many issues that require objective, intelligent and coordinated action by centralized governance. The assumption is questionable on all fronts, but perhaps most importantly it violates Constitutional provisions.

Just like a cancer, Government continues to grow, absorbing nutrients that the body can use and replacing productive cells with malignant ones that eventually destroy the host.

In his Inaugural Address *Ronald Reagan* stated: "In this current crisis government is not the solution to the problem; government is the problem." Here we are four decades later, in another economic crisis with a much larger government, and still no solutions. Could it be that *Reagan* was right? In a 2012 *Gallup* survey 61% of respondents indicated they felt the Government was doing too much that could better be handled by individuals and businesses, while 31% (probably government employees) responded the Government should do more to solve the country's problems (the remainder of respondents had a "mixed" or "depends" reply).

When the framers of the Constitution began to debate the role of the government in our new country they obviously considered their oppressive experience with the *British* government. This must have influenced their decision to severely limit the role of a national government in the nascent nation. As a result the U.S. government has limited Constitutional authority. The primary purpose of the Federal Government was defined as:

--Defend the Country
--Establish a currency system
--Deliver the mail
--Protect individual rights

And the tenth Amendment to the *Bill of Rights* specified that all other powers are reserved "to the states respectively, or to the people."

Well, we do have military forces to defend our shores, a monetary system with which to transact business, and a *U.S. Postal Service* to deliver the mail. The government's record regarding protection of individual rights has been questionable.

Let's explore this a little further. Even in these limited areas of primary responsibility has the government abused, expanded, or neglected its role?

Defend the Country

As we reviewed earlier in this book, our adventurous military is spread throughout the world similar to the armies of ancient empires. Defending the shores has expanded to a world-wide presence with policing, preemptive, and interventionist practices. At present our role may be described as: "destabilizing," "nation building," "regime toppling," and of course, "defending," not only our country but others.

Establish a Currency System

The "Almighty Dollar" was a common expression for many years. It's not heard as frequently these days as the value of the currency is eroded by inflation and weakened by debt and short-sighted monetary policies. Again, the government doesn't seem to be exercising this primary role in a responsible and effective fashion.

Deliver the Mail

This role appears to be exercised in a reasonably responsible fashion. Sure it's costly, and yes it's been semi-privatized, and encountered major competition by private delivery services (notably *UPS* and *FedEx*) but it functions and is quite efficient. It provides doorstep service to almost every address in America six days a week and handles more items each day than *Fedex* does in a year.

Protect Individual Rights

This area has been troublesome to say the least. Progress has been slow and fitful. The Government seems reticent to support individual members of minority groups and regularly violates the rights of perhaps a majority. As we discussed earlier in the book the anti-terrorism, *Homeland Security* and *National Security Administration* initiatives have ostensibly provided "cover" for surveillance or investigation of individuals and groups by federal agencies and law enforcement.

A Poor Record

Our record is pathetic. Of the Governmental functions explicitly authorized by the Constitution only one is without question being faithfully executed – delivery of mail in accordance with the inscription on the *New York* General Post Office: "Neither snow nor rain nor heat nor gloom of night stays these couriers from the swift completion of their appointed rounds."

Federal Agencies that are Useless or Counterproductive

Useless Federal agencies are almost legendary and far better than those that do major harm. The framers of the Constitution would, I'm certain, roll over in their graves if they were aware of how grotesquely bloated, corrupt and inept the Government has become. The dimensions, scope and reach of our Government is almost inconceivable, even when compared with dictatorships or socialist regimes. The Government intrudes into every aspect of your life. To provide some context I thought it might be helpful to look at some of the largest and most problematic Federal Agencies.

Let's start with the granddaddy of them all the *Department of Defense*. This is the agency which is responsible for defending the nation, by force if required. Formerly it was called the *War Department*, and that might be a better mission. I'm not sure how much of their massive over half-a-trillion-dollar budget is spent defending *this* country but we know it's a world-wide operation with many secret projects.

The *Department of Health and Human Services'* Director, *Kathleen Sebelius* capsulizes her department's goal as follows: "Our goal is for all Americans to live healthier, more prosperous, and more productive lives" (hhs.gov). It's nice to have expansive goals and big dreams, but the $892 billion budget hasn't accomplished that for me. How about you? The agency has many relationships with Big Pharma, Big Health and big pesticide companies. Hopefully the boundaries are well constructed and these alliances are more beneficial to the people than profitable to these partners.

The *Department of Agriculture* is another behemoth with strong ties to pesticide, fertilizer, genetic engineering and many other industries. Their mission is: "We provide leadership on food, agriculture, natural resources, rural development, nutrition, and related issues based on sound public policy, the best available science, and efficient management" (USDA.gov). They also manage the huge and rapidly expanding *SNAP* (Supplemental Nutrition Assistance [food stamp]) Program. With a $155 billion *USDA* budget we should have the best food at the lowest prices.

The hundred billion dollars we spend annually on *Homeland Security* may be money well spent, but probably not. Every time I see airport *TSA* searching an 80 year old grandmother or frisking a 10 year old child I don't feel any safer.

DOE, the Department of Education spends $55 billion annually. As a consequence of their educational leadership we have dumbed down the curriculum and developed a workforce unfit to compete with our advanced world counterparts.

The *Department of Justice* is responsible for our other war – the War on Drugs – and for such fascinating operations as "Fast and Furious," aptly named as taxpayers are furious with them for concocting such a lame-brained scheme. Their $13.8 billion budget is a fraction of the amount we spend supporting all the spy agencies like the *CIA*, *FBI*, *NSA*, etc.

FEMA, notable for their handling of disasters like hurricanes *Katrina* and *Sandy* gets an annual allotment of over $13 billion.

The *IRS* with their emphasis of individual taxpayers and small businesses while ignoring major culprits and targeting political enemies, also has a $13+ billion budget.

And the *EPA* gets a measly $8 and a half billion despite their not-so-commendable action on the Gulf Oil Spill and numerous unethical experimentations.

Are Major Cuts in Order?

Now that we've reviewed the highlights of some of our Government's major and most well-known agencies let's look at some others. *Republican* Presidential Candidate *Ron Paul* in 2011 proposed federal employee pay cuts and the elimination of several federal departments including: *Energy, Housing and Urban Development, Commerce,* and *Interior.* Also, *TSA (Transportation Security Administration)*, and a small program called *COPS (Community Oriented Policing Services)*. He also suggested eliminating one of the largest agencies-- the *Education Department*, and providing block grants to states for most health and human services programs including *USDA*'s *SNAP* (Food Stamps) program. *Paul* didn't make it out of the primaries and probably didn't receive many votes from well-organized government employees.

Many voters liked his approach whereas others thought his plans were too radical. I found him a breath of fresh air on the political landscape, someone self-assured enough to aggressively challenge the status quo.

Whether it's major cuts or major restructuring a serious in-depth analysis of the value and impact of government spending programs is in order. It takes a fearless leader to challenge the bureaucrats. They're smart, politically savvy and resistant to change.

Perhaps Government agencies should take a cue from the popular TV show, *"Biggest Loser."* On that program obese individuals compete for the opportunity to work with an expert personal trainer for one year. The trainer establishes weight loss goals and the trainer and subject jointly implement a rigorous program of diet and exercise. Obviously some government agencies have become too fat. Their waist (or more accurately "waste") has become large and flabby from years of neglect and misplaced priorities. They have grown too large to become fit, healthy and effective. Could they learn a lesson from the *"Biggest Loser?"* I say yes. Put them on a regimen of austerity and improvement. Of course the measurement of improvement isn't as simple as a needle on a scale.

Private enterprise ascertains their health by measures of "growth and profitability." In the public sector it should be just the opposite—the leanest agencies at the lowest costs, consistent with quality public service. But that isn't the way it works. Under the current system agency heads view budget and employee growth as a measure of success. Typically the larger agencies have the most clout and their directors enjoy the biggest paychecks.

An incentive program for a new cost and service efficiency model would be required to change managers' mindsets from the current model of "spend everything" and "get more" in the budget to one directed toward: achieve savings, improve efficiency and promote cost-effectiveness.

The Potential for Savings

The potential for savings is enormous. The most recent *Census Department* information (released 8/13/13 covering data through 3/2011) reports a total of 22.2 million government employees at all levels. That is not a misprint. The total U.S. workforce ranges between 140-150 million. This means a phenomenal ratio of approximately 1:7; government employee: private sector employee.

[181]

One in seven of all employed people in the country work for the government! The largest category is employed in education with over one-half of the total; the next biggest category is law enforcement.

The military also employs millions of people either directly or indirectly (through contractors). Former Secretary of Labor *Robert Reich* calls this "America's Biggest Jobs Program" (*Christian Science Monitor*, 8/13/10) and "an insane way to keep Americans employed."

An interesting comparison can be made between Government jobs and manufacturing jobs. In 1960 there were 22,166,000 employees in the manufacturing sector vs. 8,307,000 employed by the government.

Today, in a shocking reversal, 22,200,000 are employed by the government while less than 11,000,000 work in manufacturing.

As we learned in Chapter Two, and other places in this book, these government employees are generally highly compensated employees. Clearly it is time to initiate a concerted effort directed at how much government can be reduced. The possibility of saving hundreds of billions, or as candidate *Ron Paul* indicated, a $trillion or more is quite real.

Wars

Your Government has a history of losing wars. Not the military type but the social ones. The bureaucrats love to declare "war" on social problems. It's a powerful metaphor indicating that we're serious about eliminating a problem (opponent) and consolidates resources, financial assets and support. Of course it seldom works but it helps immensely in building bureaucracies. There are many examples: The *War on Poverty*, *War on Drugs*, *War on Cancer*, *War on Hunger*, *War on Drunk Driving*, *War on Teen Pregnancy*, and *War on Terrorism*. Most of these wars are never-ending, or unwinnable and counter-productive like the *War on Poverty* which began in 1965 and will soon celebrate its 50th Anniversary, with no victory in sight!

The Government never met a program it didn't like. They will keep finding ways to create bigger - not better - more costly programs to address evey conceivable issue. The government always finds a way to remain a growth industry even during economic downturns. Come to think of it, economic downturns are opportunities for more programs ostensibly designed to fix these difficulties. They make it their job to get money from us to build empires for them. As long as we let them.

Downsizing?

Given the government's exceptionally poor record of fixing social and economic problems does anyone in their right frame of mind really trust them to fix things? Does big government fix big problems or spend big bucks creating even bigger problems – like the cost of employing the problem solvers/creators and the unintended consequences for the citizenry? Maybe it's time to try the opposite approach and reduce the size and scope of government intervention.

How many departments, agencies, functions and employees can be reduced or eliminated? Obviously we would want to approach this intelligently, not by using a "meat axe" technique. Besides, reductions should consider the impact on targeted agencies and staff. Severance packages, attrition, interagency transfers, private-sector partner placements, etc. should all be considered. A smooth, yet efficient and meaningful transition would be best and less stressful on the economy.

It has just become out of control and we can't continue "business as usual." The taxpayers are weary of supporting massive government agencies, consisting of thousands of well-paid employees who often appear to be producing nothing of real value but create regulations that, in turn, result in higher costs.

[183]

Lessons from the Impasse

Perhaps there really is opportunity in crisis. When the political crisis of October 2013 resulted in a partial shutdown and a frightening prospect of national debt default the public gained a quick, much-needed education on the enormous size and overwhelming dysfunctionality of our government.

We saw that rather than rising to the occasion, our leaders became less able to problem-solve and ever-more petty and vindictive. We were informed that with over two million federal employees the U.S. government was the largest employer in the world! We learned that the White House had over 1,700 staff and the first lady even had ghost-writer employees to produce her "tweets" on *Twitter*. We realized that the government had not had a budget since 2009 and they were operating on a series of "continuing resolutions." We discovered that it was more costly to close open air monuments like the *WWII Memorial* than it would have been to leave it open. We were reminded that following the painful and protracted shutdown in 1986 none other than *Bill Clinton* had exclaimed in frustration: "The era of big government is over!" But here we were seventeen years later with an even bigger and more dysfunctional one.

Can the Government be taught to Dance?

The massive increase in the size and scope of the federal government and their consequent impact on every aspect of the nation and its people should not be underestimated. As we've seen they can impact our financial future (employment, housing, income, retirement, investments, taxes, etc.), as well as our rights, freedoms and securities. Their impact is felt, for better or worse, by everyone.

Sometimes it's hard to connect the dots between government policy and the average person's life. Your leaders like that.

[184]

Aside from blaming the other politician(s) or party they love to blame other countries, international events, a poor economy, macro-cycles, the behavior of specific groups of people or entities (welfare recipients, drug dealers, Wall Street, corporate greed, etc.).

What they fail to acknowledge is their role in all of these factors. You see, the results of the heavy hand of the government are difficult to define and explain. And we never know what secret alliances and interests they cultivate and exploit.

It makes me think: What tricks do the politicians have in store for us? And, of course, what havoc will it wreak.

Some 20 years ago there was a business management book titled *Teaching the Elephant to Dance* (by *James Belasco, PhD*) examining the challenges in making giant corporations more nimble, adaptive, proactive, anticipatory, competitive and successful. Could some of the insights, principles, strategies and techniques which apply in the private sector work in the public arena?

Grace and large mass don't often mesh. Large size is often associated with clumsiness and slow movement. Do you think our government has learned to dance? Apparently not. Do they have the capacity? Perhaps. But they may need discipline, diet, and focus to do it. And they'll have to break the shackles of decades of conditioning. We have an excellent "Mission Statement," "Goals," "Values," and operations guide provided by the *Constitution* and the visionaries who created this nation. For the most part they provided us with "big picture" ideas and documents; empowering, aspirational, moral and motivational. These guides are also flexible and forward looking enough to serve the nation throughout its development and maturity. However, I doubt if we'll ever see the Government on *Dancing with the Stars,* or even more unlikely the *Biggest Loser.* The government has learned too many bad habits, gotten way out of shape and forgotten the discipline necessary to win.

[185]

Meanwhile the challenges have grown and the competition has been taking dancing lessons and practicing rigorously. They recognize we're not the graceful, disciplined, motivated, determined, focused, adroit, smart competitor we used to be. As a result, on the world stage we may stumble and fall, get low marks and be voted out!

Too harsh, you say? Probably. We may continue to rank among the finalists for many years, but we need to watch our backs!

The message is one of going back to our basic values of hard work, discipline, motivation, and recapture our strength and confidence. We have "natural talent," and extensive resources to help us. We have millions of supporters, too. The trainers and coaches may be in short supply, but I have no doubt they will emerge when their leadership is most required and appreciated.

Are we Becoming More Socialist?

Americans like to point fingers at European countries as examples of socialist states where the governments have a much larger role and there's a "cradle to grave" state-sponsored welfare mentality. Are we really that different? As it turns out, we're not, as least by some measures (as outlined in a 2012 report by the *Manhattan Institute*). We are moving towards a socialist style system, albeit without all the benefits. Yes, we are growing a comparably sized government without providing the same high level of services.

It's almost the worst of both worlds. Our Government is extraordinarily expensive yet exceptionally inefficient at proving quality services. They can't even agree on a budget for God's sake. They just want *more*.

If the Government had a theme song it would probably be something like "*More More More*" from *Last Days of Disco*, especially the lines:

"More, more, more
How do you like it, how do you like it?
More, more, more
How do you like it, how do you like it?
More, more, more"

Just as in the disco song, your government always craves *more*. More programs, more taxes, more employees and more power, and even more strangely we seem willing to feed that addiction.

We pay a similar proportion of national *GDP* as some E.U. countries (when 5.6% is included for private health insurance) and are close to their aggregate average. In *Europe* as in the U.S. government (including State and Local) sucks up almost 50% of *GDP*!

And the trends at opposite sides of the *Atlantic* are in opposite directions too. As *European* governments shrink as a proportion of their economy ours is expanding. The Government to GDP ratio for the *Euro* area was 49.3% in 2012; in the U.S. it was 46.8%.

Sweden at one point had the most expansive social welfare system and was the "poster child" for *European* socialism. However their ratio has declined from 68% in 1993, to 47% in 2012. A remarkable accomplishment.

What should we do? Is this the path we want to take? Can the private sector afford to subsidize a government that absorbs half of *GDP*? We better start rethinking our priorities and direction. Otherwise, a massive government consuming over half the national *GDP* is our future.

A wise and frugal Government,
which shall restrain men from injuring one another,
which shall leave them otherwise free to regulate their
own pursuits of industry and improvement,
and shall not take from the mouth of labor the bread it
has earned. This is the sum of good government....

--Thomas Jefferson

Promising too much can be as cruel as caring too little.

--William J. Clinton

Let us all take more responsibility, not only for
ourselves and our families but for our communities
and our country.

--William J. Clinton

[188]

Chapter Twenty

Social Consequences

In Physics we learned "for every action there's an equal and opposite reaction," in Biology it's "stimulus/response" and in Psychology its Operant and Respondent Behavior. It seems the natural order is to expect a reaction from your actions. Too bad our leaders forgot this simple principle.

We've looked at several of the many tricks the Government plays on us. However, they can't expect to keep playing forever - that's unrealistic. They can improve their game-playing skills while we scratch our heads in disbelief and amazement. They can embrace new technologies, social media, and co-opt the mainstream media. They can improve their rhetoric and presentation skills. The current crop is certainly more polished in front of a camera or microphone than their predecessors. Of course at some point public tolerance for these techniques will evaporate and the electorate will only be satisfied with substance. This culture of manipulation, greed and corruption will become intolerable and we'll witness the "End Game." A "Tipping Point" as *Malcom Gladwell* refers to it; a capitulation.

As the majority of Americans become poorer and more disillusioned they will demand REAL CHANGE. Not the bogus and elusive kind that politicians always promise. *Fear* as a political strategy will lose some of its allure and no longer garner support.

Fear Mongering

We've been tricked too many times. Fear of the *"Commies,"* the *Muslims*, the *Blacks*, the *Immigrants*, *Red China*, the *Iraqis*, the *Iranians*, *Syrians* and *North Koreans*; the *Tea Party*, the *Republicans*, *Democrats*, *Libertarians*, the *Rappers*, the *Gays* and the *Atheists*; *Hollywood*, the *NRA*, etc. Do you want me to go on? I suspect not, especially after reading all the *Weiner* jokes in Chapter 16. I'm sure you get the picture-- *We live in fear*. Much of it orchestrated by politicians and special interests. And as we've seen, there's big money in fear-mongering. Money for politicians, corporations, individuals, armaments, government, etc. The Government's motto seems to be: "Keep Fear Alive!"

Those fear tactics are diversionary. They are also "divisionary;" they divide us as a people. Remember the military strategy "Divide and Conquer?" Our real fear is much closer at hand - a dysfunctional and oppressive government and misguided, corrupt politicians.

Millions of our neighbors are unemployed, underemployed, hungry, broke and discouraged. Now there's *real fear*! How long can we continue to have millions of people excluded from meaningful participation in our capitalistic system? How long can we endure millions locked up in jails and prisons, mostly for ridiculous drug charges, or minor offenses, while the really big crooks are wining and dining in *Washington*? How long will we tolerate billions in bailouts for crooked bankers, billions in subsidies for favored industries or projects, billions for war, and billions to promote a domestic "police state" where our government routinely abuses our Rights? It's all screwed up!

A Policy of Appeasement

We have a strategy of pandering and patronizing the poor to keep them appeased and believing the Government is on their side while the real largess is funneled to the wealthy and connected.

It's a good trick! Make the masses believe we're trying to help them, keep the middle class marginally satisfied, shift capital and jobs overseas; concentrate wealth in the hands of a few and encourage those beneficiaries of the process to financially support the corrupt politicians to keep the game going and the money flowing. All the while spending the country into oblivion so that there isn't much of a future for the young, and future generations.

A "Ticking Time Bomb?"

The model for this nation was based on freedom, opportunity, and economic progress. The current reality is a retreat in all of these key areas. How will our citizenry react when they discover it's not a temporary setback, but instead it's a structural and corruption problem. We/ve always experienced economic cycles. Booms and crashes, panics and runaway growth, recessions and depressions, and recoveries. But the overall trajectory was an upward one with most generations doing better than the previous one. We discussed this "American Dream" in Chapter Four.

This time appears different. Have we lost our "Mojo?"

The big movements in this country have generally centered on human rights: Voting Rights, Civil Rights, Women's Rights, Gay Rights. And protests, for example: anti-war, anti-Wall Street (e.g. "Occupy Wall Street"). However, there is a common thread through all of these issues—the Government! They make the policies, the laws, require enforcement, and adjudicate conflicts. However, we haven't seen many big anti-Government protests in recent history.

When large numbers of people realize their Government is not adequately representing them, or their interests, instead of small, single-issue movements we may see a groundswell of dissatisfaction and disenchantment with the "system."

Politicians should be aware of the perils associated with arrogance, detachment and insensitivity to the plight of the average American. The finger-pointing between the parties has worn thin. The trick of blaming the other party for the big problems doesn't wash. We've witnessed both parties fail at governance and leadership too many times. The close ties to moneyed interests and the distant ties with the general population, are obvious. It's also obvious that our elected leaders are "out for themselves." For the politicians it's less about "public service" than being "self-serving."

Signs of Unraveling

Look at some recent headlines and see if the system is functional or unraveling: "Elderly Increasingly Go Hungry," "Black Youth in Peril," "Middle Class Continues To Shrink," "Wages Stagnate," "Home Ownership Declining," and "Murder-Rate: Once Again on Increase."

Also, "Graduates Can't Find Employment," "More Young Adults Moving Back With Parents," "Cost of Healthcare Prohibitive," "Average Vehicle Now Over 10 Years," "American Dream Lost?" "Net-Worth Declines," "The Disillusioned Generation," "Are Millennials The Screwed Generation?"

Aren't you tired of our politicians spending their energies fund-raising, travelling, vacationing, in-fighting, posturing, evading, and not taking responsibility? Each time a politician takes office he blames his predecessor, or the opposition party, or Congress, or the President, or the terrorists, or the phase of the moon. Anything to avoid taking responsibility! Where's the *Truman* mentality- "The Buck Stops Here!" - when we need it?

Social Protest and Civil Disintegration

If the same trajectory continues there will be outrage and upheaval. The continuing concentration of wealth in the hands of a few, the shrinking financial prospects for the many, an apparently detached government, a well-established system of political manipulation through special interest/government financial coziness are elements all reaching a crescendo.

In this Country we've witnessed social movements, anti war protests, social equality protests, major Civil Rights and Racial Equality protests, demonstrations and movements, Occupy Wall Street demonstrations, etc. But we haven't yet witnessed a general Economic Inequality Movement. One is coming, however. As sure as inequalities of any type prod and energize social movements, rapidly growing economic inequalities have an even greater potential for involvement and participation. And this issue hits home with at least 80% of the population. If we examine the disparities in depth it could resonate with 99% of the populous. This could be the most significant movement in our Country's history.

[193]

Americans are well aware of the problem and weary of the political tricks. We've been led to believe that the economic disruptions are temporary, and recovery is underway. But the average wage-earner knows this isn't true. The wealthy, large corporations, banking conglomerates and the government may try to resist or pretend to be supportive, but it won't work. All it will take is a catalyst—another downturn or a charismatic protest leader and the frustrations will swell into major opposition to our leaders and established government programs.

Chapter Twenty-one

You've Got Rights!

You have rights! Now go out and exercise them! Perhaps a "refresher" is in order. In this chapter we explore the "Bill of Rights" its intent and content; its purpose and importance.

The Constitution includes a list of rights for individual citizens. You probably learned these, or perhaps even had to memorize them in school. The first ten amendments to the Constitution are the *Bill of Rights*. The people responsible for founding this country and the leaders and thinkers who wrote the Constitution were protective of the individual and concerned that a power-hungry or tyrannical government might attempt to abridge the rights of the people and impinge or restrict our freedoms. So essentially the Bill of Rights is intended to protect us from our government by clarifying our rights *and* granting privileges to our government. This is an important distinction: We *have the rights* and we (the people) grant certain privileges to our government(s) to protect these rights. This was a powerful act and remains a vital protection.

The Executive and Legislative branches of our government are supposed to respect our (*God*-given) rights, and if they don't, the Judicial Branch (Supreme Court) is there to make sure they do! So, it works this way. We have rights and we allow the government to perform certain actions on our behalf. Primarily the privileges we allow the government to have are those intended to enforce the respect of our life, liberty and property. On the following page is a concise, considerably abbreviated outline of the Bill of Rights.

Bill of Rights
(a really abbreviated version)

1	Freedom of religion, speech, press, assembly, and petition.
2	Right to keep and bear arms.
3	No quartering of soldiers.
4	Freedom from unreasonable searches and seizures.
5	Right to due process of law, freedom from self-incrimination, double jeopardy.
6	Rights of accused persons, e.g., right to a speedy and public trial.
7	Right of trial by jury.
8	Freedom from excessive bail, cruel and unusual punishments.
9	Other rights of the people. *
10	Powers reserved to the states. **

*the people have many additional rights not enumerated in the Constitution
**power flows from people to the states, and ultimately to the Federal government, but it is a revocable granting of privilege.

Q: After reading the previous chapters, how many of these basic rights do you really have?
A: All of them.

Which one(s) is our government trying to restrict or curtail? Which ones are under attack? Think about it. Your government may be "Out to Get You!" Now let's look at each "Right" in more detail and see how we're doing as a country in maintaining and protecting these rights.

OUT TO GET YOU

We've already touched on several in previous chapters, but a brief assessment is definitely in order. Just for fun let's assign a letter grade to each Constitutional Right. Subjective perhaps, but see if you agree.

REPORT CARD

BOR #1 Freedom of Speech...**D-**
This number one human right in a free society is definitely under attack. The revelations about government eavesdropping on your phone calls, perusing your emails, and monitoring your library books, internet search history, etc. assuredly means they're OTGY. It is closely tied to BOR #4.

BOR #2 Right to Bear Arms..**C-**
Call them fanatics, but the NRA is protecting your Constitutional Right to own a firearm. We can quibble about the types of arms ordinary citizens should be allowed to possess, or the background search of license applicants, these are reasonable debates. But the right to bear arms means you can defend yourself and your country by force when necessary and it's under attack.

BOR #3 No quartering of soldiers. ....**A**
When was the last time you were asked to house a soldier who wasn't an invited relative or friend.

BOR #4 Freedom from Unreasonable Searches and Seizures.....................**D**
Warrantless searches have increased, and appear to be condoned. "Stop and Frisk" procedures are in place in numerous jurisdictions. In New York a Judge recently curtailed the practice by *NYPD* and has required improved policies and procedures. Profiling continues to be practiced in numerous locales. And electronic surveillance through use of cameras and drones regularly invading our privacy. But the biggest intrusion is *NSA* surveillance of Internet activities of citizens.

BOR #5 Right to Due Process..**C**
The protections included in this provision are often abridged with regard to suspected terrorism, but is largely intact in most other cases.

BOR #6 Rights of Accused Persons..**C**
Another problem area, particularly in drug or terrorism cases and Court trial delays for others.

BOR #7 Trial by Jury...**B**
Again, jurisdictions and protections are in question with regard to international terrorism suspects.

BOR #9 & 10...**N/A**

The **GPA**: 2.0, only a **C**!

If you're a parent you might be upset if your child brought home a report card like this one. If you're a student you would undoubtedly vow to do better. And you might reflect on how lucky you were to get an "easy A" on BOR#3, otherwise it would be an even lower GPA.

If you're the Government you may think "that's not so bad" or not pay it any attention! If you're a U.S. citizen you should be thinking, "I expect straight A's." In fact, that is precisely the benchmark I used in assigning grades to these first ten Constitutional Amendments. The comparison is not with other nations, after all there is no Bell Curve for human rights. It's a comparison with our own expressed ideals and goals. We shouldn't be aiming for mediocrity but for excellence and our ambition should be to achieve that.

Had the comparison been with other nations we certainly would have scored higher. In fact, in many, perhaps the majority of countries, my freedom of speech would not have encompassed the ability to write and publish a book like this one. I recognize what a marvel this is and we should not take it for granted. But unless it's defended and people are outraged at violations we can watch our Constitutional Rights gradually wither away.

Ironically it is in the name of Freedom that our government is taking away our freedoms! The logic is something akin to: We have to protect our free country so we can't permit people to freely act, speak, inquire, research, interact with others, etc, because they might say or do something which would result in the loss of freedom! Say, what?!

The framers of the Constitution recognized that the people hold the power, although increasingly the government acts as though they do, and that they let us enjoy some rights as they see fit. It's all backwards, isn't it? (For a brief synopsis of the Constitution itself check the Appendix where you will find a summary of what I believe to be the essence of the document. It's very short, on purpose, and I encourage you to read the entire Constitution, especially if it's been a long time since you last did.

At times in our history we have ignored or suspended the rights of our citizens and downright trampled our constitutional protections. This has always proven to be a shameful mistake.

Although the brilliant and noble minds that created our government recognized the equality of all they didn't always practice it. Several signers of the Constitution were slave owners, and considered blacks their property, not their equals. This troubling legacy continued for generations and its sickening residue remains with us today. However, our Constitution and the Bill of Rights represent an ideal to which we must all be committed.

Some would argue "it's like the *Bible* and shouldn't be taken literally" Others are traditionalists who believe in the sanctity of the document. After all, well over two thousand years the *"Ten Commandments"* still apply, don't they?

The codification of your rights as part of our Constitution is a major safeguard for us all. Don't allow the erosion of these protections through ignorance of them, tacit acceptance of their unequal application, or abuse by slimy politicians.

By now you probably recognize that our nation is in a precarious circumstance. One major event could topple it. Especially economic events such as the *USD* losing reserve currency status, or crushing debt soaking up most governmental revenues, or something we considered unlikely until October, 2013 -- failure to raise the debt ceiling and defaulting on our national debt.

It could be a massive technology failure; one that renders the internet useless for an extended period. Or it could be a natural disaster such as a major earthquake in California (the world's sixth largest economy). It might be that economic inequality would destroy the fabric of our society. Or it could be that our government becomes so intrusive, oppressive and callous in observing our rights that people refuse to support it.

It's like a house of cards, propped up by fragile, precariously placed pieces of laminated paper, ready to topple at the first unexpected ill wind.

You're probably thinking that could never happen. The U.S. is too big, strong and powerful. But the fact is: *It always happens.*

Every great country and society, every system has a period of growth and ascendancy, then peaks and declines.

Historians recall the *Roman Empire, Mongol Empire, Russian Empire, Holy Roman Empire, British Empire, Han Dynasty, Byzantine Empire, Persian Empire and Ottoman Empire*. Recent history has seen dominant empires, as well, but the cycles of dominance appear to be getting shorter.

Turchin and *Nefedov*, in their book *Secular Cycles* have analyzed the collapses of great societies and confirm it doesn't take place overnight. Their theory includes multiple factors such as wages, state finances and socio-political instability. Although their study concentrated on agrarian societies the model is clearly applicable to industrialized nations. They trace economic phases from expansion to stagflation, though crisis to depression/intercycle until the State fails. If they're right, it looks as though we've gone through expansion to stagflation and are flirting with the final stages.

Just as the 19th century belonged to the *British*, and the 20th belonged to us, the history of the 21st century is just beginning to be written.

OUT TO GET YOU

When even one American -
who has done nothing wrong -
is forced by fear to shut his mind
and close his mouth -
then all Americans are in peril.

--Harry S. Truman

If you can't convince them, confuse them.

--Harry S. Truman

Those who want the Government to regulate matters
of the mind and spirit
are like men who are so afraid of being murdered
that they commit suicide to
avoid assassination.

--Harry S. Truman

Chapter Twenty-two

What Does Real Leadership Look Like?

It's been so long since we've seen real political leadership we may have difficulty remembering what it looks like. Let me remind you: It looks decisive, principled, visionary, and proactive. It places the country first, no matter the position our level of the officeholder. Public Service is a role that requires integrity and commitment.

Historians generally rank Presidential leadership in a variety of factors: E.g. Public Persuasion, Crisis Leadership, Economic Management, Moral Authority, International Relations, Relations with Congress, Vision, Pursuit of Equal Justice, and Administrative Skills. Obviously the context of the times during which the President served will have an impact on that leader's legacy.

Historian Rankings

All lists place *Lincoln* at the top, and *James Buchanan* at the bottom, so apparently excellence in leadership (or lack thereof) is universally recognized. *Washington* is typically ranked second and both *Roosevelt*'s (*Franklin D, and Theodore*) rank extremely high. *Truman* and *Jefferson* are winners, while *(Andrew) Johnson, Pierce, Harrison* and *Harding* don't fare well.

[203]

Among recent Presidents: *Dwight D. Eisenhower, John F. Kennedy, Ronald Reagan,* and *Lyndon B. Johnson,* were superior, ranking in the top quartile; *George Bush (Sr.), and Bill Clinton,* weren't bad either, with an average rating; *Gerald Ford, Jimmy Carter* and *Richard Nixon* faring a little worse, and *George W. Bush* bringing up the rear. It's too early for history to judge *Barack Obama*'s presidential performance, although his public approval ratings have been less than stellar.

In his book "The President as Leader" *Michael Siegel* boils the array of presidential behaviors and attitudes down to four leadership qualities that "define excellence in the White House."

1. A Compelling Vision
2. Ability to Implement the Vision
3. A Few Major Goals
4. Understand Decision-Making

Reagan would score high on these qualities. He knew what he wanted to accomplish and understood how to get it done. *Carter*, on the other hand, couldn't decide what to do, and as a result squandered his political capital and a more favorable place in history by going in too many directions at once.

A Good Checklist

Now that we know how academicians and historians assess Presidential leadership we have a good checklist for our own decision making when voting for a candidate. When making up our minds we would do well to disregard the trivial and focus on the important. Wouldn't it be better to select a potential *Lincoln* instead of a likely *Buchanan*? Oftentimes we make our ballot decisions emotionally rather than analytically. Or we detach and become discouraged or disinterested. However, as we've seen throughout this book, that could be an important mistake, as our Country's leadership may in some measure impact your personal future and the future of your families and loved ones. This is not abstract; it's real.

A bad leader can spell big trouble!

It is to be regretted that the rich and powerful too often bend the acts of government to their own selfish purposes.

--Andrew Jackson

America's present need is not heroics but healing; not nostrums but normalcy; not revolution but restoration.

--Warren G. Harding

The ship of democracy, which has weathered all storms, may sink through the mutiny of those on board.

--Grover Cleveland

The goal to strive for is a poor government but a rich people.

--Andrew Johnson

Chapter Twenty-three

What Can You Do?

You're the one that counts! The government was created to support, serve, and protect you. Government officials will come and go. You've seen many of their faces in your lifetime. Although I didn't call this a trick, there's a huge one underlying the discussion in this chapter. They've convinced you you're powerless to change anything.

It seems hopeless, doesn't it? How can an individual change what's happening? Well, it's always been about individuals. People with a passion, a concern, a dream. Think of *Martin Luther King, Jr.,* the Founding Fathers, the religious figures, Think of *Gandhi, Jesus Christ, Thomas Jefferson,* and *Rosa Parks.* Think of the inventors like *Edison,* industrialists like *Henry Ford,* financiers like *Carnegie* and *Rockefeller.* Think of the Presidents like *Lincoln, Roosevelt, Reagan,* and *Truman.* Think of the creators like *Steve Jobs* and *Bill Gates.* Now, you're probably thinking "but he just mentioned some names that I think did more harm than good." And, yes, that's the way it works. Leaders and dreamers don't always fit our preconceived notions of heroism or altruism. They don't always do what we want, like, appreciate, or value. But they do something! And they'll continue to do something whether you like it or not. The good ones benefit from our support. The bad ones benefit from our apathy.

Your government has a great deal of power to improve or disrupt your life. We see that they can create wars, on our own people like the "War on Drugs," internationally like the "War on Terrorism," or real wars like the wars and armed conflicts that we constantly engage in. Your government can manipulate or influence the economy, your livelihood and your prosperity.

They can make interest rates higher or lower, credit liberal or difficult to obtain. They can spy on you, your family and neighbors, and they can harass you with agencies like the *NSA* or the *IRS*.

Far from being a free society, we're increasingly subject to intrusions, restrictions, legal interference, and fear. Yes, many of us fear our government, and often the sources or reasons for that fear are far too real. A positive sign is the extremely strong backlash against government surveillance of our citizenry. Congress hasn't experienced this level of public concern in a while. It is proof that our leaders can't just take away all of our freedoms and privacy. Congress actually responded by defunding the NSA's expanded surveillance program as it should have. But how many *Snowden*'s do we have? How would we know about these goings on?

Do we need government? Certainly! Does it have to be as large? Probably not. Could it be more efficient? Definitely. More responsive to the needs of the citizenry? For sure! It seems like we're on a path to decay. Either we begin rebuilding now or we wait for complete disintegration. Perhaps we have to follow the course outlined by Alcoholics Anonymous and "bottom out." But what if we can't recover? What if we succumb to our addictions and misbehaviors?

Most of us are too busy posting pictures or platitudes on *Facebook*, or inane incomplete thoughts on *Twitter* to get involved in politics or monitor what's happening in our government. With some notable exceptions we seldom use these technologies to express political, social, or economic thoughts. No, "keep it light" seems to be the practice of all but a few passionate or activist individuals.

[208]

Wouldn't want to offend anyone. Wouldn't want to challenge anyone to think. Besides some prospective employer or government agent might be snooping. Wouldn't want to appear too serious, or committed, or involved or serious, or radical or conservative, or liberal or interested. If you're one of those who is more vocal – congrats.

So what can you do?

Get to know the people who represent you in Congress: The Senators and House of Representatives members for your State and District. If you don't know, make it your job to find out. Go to www.whoismyrepresentative.com. At that site you can quickly access the information by Zip Code and/or State. Access their official website(s) and introduce yourself by sending an email expressing your pleasure or dissatisfaction with their performance. Be sure to mention issues important to you, your family and your community. Don't forget to do the same with the President at www.whitehouse.com/contact. You can also find any elected official's email address at: www.usa.gov/contact/elected.

Become more informed, aware, concerned, and involved. Recognize the bias in the media and the statistical and methodological tricks the government employs when reporting data.

Look for "spin" in reports and news briefs. Try to select different channels of media information so that you won't get the same bias. Don't always select reporters and stations you agree with.

Be more skeptical. Become a more critical consumer of government created data and reports. Become more communicative, and develop your political and social views.

Write letters to the Editor. Make it a goal to become involved. Don't shy away from politics at the dinner table or with friends. Don't be reticent to express your views on social media. Realize you can make a difference.

Vote! Go to the polls on Election Day. Make yourself aware of the candidates, their backgrounds and positions. Campaign for the candidate of your choice. Support candidates with integrity (although they may be difficult to find.) Volunteer. Participate.

Don't pay any attention to the party labels especially if they start with a "R" or a "D;" in my opinion there isn't a whit of difference between the *Republicans* and the *Democrats*. They're both out to get you. Your money and your freedoms. <u>Vote for the person not the party</u>.

Share this book with your friends. At this point in our history there's a detachment from reality. Most of the population is in denial. They need to be shaken out of their somnombulance and into an actively engaged, proactive state.

Being part of a democracy, or perhaps more accurately a constitutional republic, has responsibilities as well as rights. Freedom and responsibilities go together. They're inextricably joined.

Improving the Government

How can we have a more responsible government? A government that does the right things and does them well and cost-effectively. Certainly there have been efforts directed at improving accountability, efficiency and effectiveness. The *GAO* (Government Accounting Office) is constantly reviewing and auditing government departments and functions. And "suggestion awards" programs are typically in place in government offices. But is this sufficient?

As far back as the 1980's I was fortunate to participate in a Public-Private partnership in *Los Angeles County*. I was selected to Chair the Productivity Managers Network with representatives from each county agency. The Productivity Commission was comprised of educators, entrepreneurs and successful business owners and executives.

The County *Board of Supervisors* endorsed and supported the project. The concept was to identify "best practices" that were transferrable from the private to the public sector, and between agencies within the public sector. The project was also designed to stimulate a spirit of entrepreneurship among public sector employees by creating a "Productivity Investment Fund" (PIF) to provide seed money for worthwhile proposals. (Something like an early version of "*Shark Tank*" for the public sector.)

Project advocates would present their ideas to an Investment Board empowered to grant seed money to the public employee entrepreneurs whose reward would be the opportunity to make significant change and be recognized for their efforts. Productivity Managers from each department would be responsible for spreading the word and stimulating enthusiasm.

The program was a fantastic success, saving millions in taxpayer dollars, through systems and methods improvements, and empowering stifled bureaucrats to take risks and try new things. This type of design could be, and probably has been replicated at state, county, and local levels. Some may say it won't work at the federal level. However, *L.A. County* was at that time actually larger (in population) than 42 of the 50 states and not generally known for responsible budgetary practices.

I'm certain that other jurisdictions are trying models similar to the one I just described. And I know there are many other ways to improve government. I've even considered advocating a new model for public participation in the legislative process. One that would harness the power and intelligence of the average citizen. A methodology designed to insure that special interest do not determine the outcomes of our national policy directions. This model: "A Concept for Participative Planning to Address National Priorities" is outlined in Appendix C. I hope you will take the time to check it out and let me know what you think. This may not be the *best* model for change but we need to explore hybrid or other options.

We need to gain greater participation and involvement from the people. That's the foundation of our system. And with technological advancement, interaction with the citizenry could be greatly enhanced, if there's a will.

Another recommendation would be to combine policy priority "votes" along with candidate votes in Presidential elections. Essentially the intent would be to gain public opinion information using the ballot process. This information could then be used in forming a general mandate platform for a new administration. And just as many states have referendum processes, a Referendum process could be adapted to the Federal Election process.

Just adding a few questions on the ballot that pertain to major issues confronting the nation is all that would be necessary. It's a low-cost, almost no-cost survey. Voters could rank their priorities (economic, budget, immigration, healthcare, crime, etc.).

The differences between states, counties and cities would be fascinating. The people's priorities could translate into a policy agenda for the next four years, and an assessment "report card" for elected officials.

Accountability would increase—the politicians would hate it! It would be opposed from the get-go and a real challenge to gain support for implementation. Only politicians who would support carrying out the will of the people would sign-on and that ain't many!

A nation like ours can easily deteriorate due to individual and public apathy and lack of participation. It's a durable, but at the same time fragile institution and we're counting on you to keep it healthy and effective.

Just as termites can fell a mighty tree, rot from within will destroy our nation. You're an essential part of this democracy. But you may not be for long. And it won't thrive without you.

Remember what *Lincoln* said at Gettysburg:

> It is for us the living, rather, to be dedicated here to the unfinished work which they who fought here have thus far so nobly advanced. It is rather for us to be here dedicated to the great task remaining before us -- that from these honored dead we take increased devotion to that cause for which they gave the last full measure of devotion -- that we here highly resolve that these dead shall not have died in vain -- that this nation, under God, shall have a new birth of freedom -- and that government of the people, by the people, for the people, shall not perish from the earth.

Following the most divisive period in our history, Lincoln held out hope for the future. We may never experience such a national challenge ever again. I certainly hope not.
But this nation is "built to last."

Lincoln ended his remarkable historic address with a reference to the government, emphasizing its responsibility to the people. Our political leaders need to take note, and we need to individually, and collectively renew our commitment to holding them accountable.

Whether you're a *Republican* or *Democrat*, a *Libertarian* or a *Socialist*, a *Peace and Freedom* advocate or any of the many other choices and affiliations is beside the point. There's room for all viewpoints in this magnificent and diverse nation.

Whether you concluded that your government is a trickster or not, and whether you believe we're on the right course for this time in our history or not, this book is aimed at your awareness and involvement. Whether you believe your country is a Participative Democracy or a Constitutional Republic, it requires your attention and support.

Some of the most frustrating reactions to a book like this are anger or despondency. That is not my intent or this message.

[213]

The message is: Be informed and aware, do what you can, vote and participate in the political process.

Empower yourself! I don't expect you to become a zealot, a demonstrator, or an activist, although some of you already are and others may choose that path. Just don't ignore, lie down and passively accept what bothers you about your government.

Demand change. We still have a Constitution, basic values, an intelligent and productive populous.

Finally, now that you've read almost all of the book, what do you think? Is the government Out to Get You? Are they constantly playing tricks on you? And, not just harmless pranks but serious, misguided, perhaps malicious and hurtful tricks and intentional deception? You be the judge!

As for me, I've come to my own conclusion, and it's a resounding-No! Your government is not out to get you, unless of course you're: Old, young, an employee, a business owner, an entrepreneur, female, a minority, any type of "freedom fighter," a taxpayer, gun owner, a student, an aid recipient, or an independent thinker. Reassuring isn't it?

This nation still holds the most promise of any for the future of mankind. Don't be disillusioned but be aware, and be concerned. And be involved! With people like you there's still hope.

CONCLUSION

Our Government is doing the American people a disservice. Under their stewardship they've squandered our treasure, reputation, and economic capabilities, tarnished our legacy and hocked our future. They've sold themselves to the highest bidders and compromised their integrity and ability to govern. They've surrounded themselves with cronies, contributors and political hacks. They've turned us into a middling nation no longer scoring at the top on numerous comparative measures. (Although we do rank first in percentage of population incarcerated, and military might.) Even our military prowess can't gain us respect as we're considered by many to be a "paper tiger." All of these problems are clearly evident to any informed person.

We've all heard the phrase "Beware of Greeks bearing gifts," exhorting caution when deception or ulterior motives are suspected. Here's the gist of it—

The *Trojan War* had been going on for over ten years. One day the *Greeks* moved a colossal wooden horse and left it at the gates of the city of *Troy*. The *Trojans* believed the *Greeks* had left this "gift" as a symbol of their respect for the *Trojan* warriors and an indication that they were tired of the war and would be returning home. The *Trojans* were ecstatic and moved the giant object inside the city gates. We all know what happened next. In the morning following the celebration of the war's end the *Greek* soldiers hidden within the humongous horse climbed out to slaughter the *Trojans* and open the gates for the *Greek* army that sneaked back into the area. This story may be somewhat analogous to our government's programs. Only they're already inside the gates.

OUT TO GET YOU

If the Government is giving you something you would be wise to be suspicious. Just substitute the word "Government" for the word "*Greek*:" "Beware of the *Government* bearing gifts."

There will always be "strings attached," a "price to pay," "tradeoffs," etc. As my father would say "you don't get something for nothing!" The Government's "gifts" always have ulterior motives and political intent. If they give you money you sacrifice freedom (and opportunity). If they give you healthcare you'll forego choice. If they give you protection you sacrifice freedom. If they give you welfare you sacrifice independence. If they give you food you'll see inflation at the grocery store. If they give you a dream of international peace, they'll take your sons and daughters and hock your future. If they give you a better economy they'll leave you in overwhelming debt. If they give you loans to buy a house they'll mortgage you to the hilt and inflate housing costs. If they give you money to finance your education they'll put you in lifetime debt.

In this book we examined the major issues, problems, and challenges confronting the United States. We've reconfirmed the fact that at its inception the nation was well-designed and organized to protect the rights of the citizens while limiting the role of government. This excellent governance model served us well for over two-hundred years. But we've also looked at studies, research and surveys to ascertain our current condition and found it disturbing.

We've seen examples of government intervention, influence, control and manipulation producing disruptions, distortions and unanticipated outcomes. Our excessively large, muscular, yet undisciplined and unfocused government attempts to control and manage not only our lives, but those of millions in other nations throughout the world.   Like an intoxicated bull in a china shop, damage cannot be avoided.

We've drifted far afield from our Constitutional roots into a land managed by celebrity-like politicians, unprepared and apparently uninterested in performing necessary leadership functions and failing to respect the rights and self-determination of the citizenry.

Leadership has been abdicated in favor of money and power with wealthy individuals and corporations pulling the strings of puppet politicians. We've watched our international reputation decline, our economy falter, our freedoms abridged, and our futures become less certain.

We've seen other nations prosper at our expense, a small percentage of our population control most of the nation's wealth, and a growing underclass of consisting of discouraged underemployed or unemployed individuals. We've seen our powerhouse economy become a minimum-wage service economy, while other countries develop manufacturing and technological prowess. We've watched the politicians play budget and economic tricks, social games, and scare tactics.

The Government isn't entirely to blame for our sadly deteriorating situation. Of course we live in a more competitive world. Sure automation and technology have eviscerated and altered the workforce. Yes, there are cyclical forces at play. Certainly the electorate has become more detached and pessimistic. But these factors don't excuse our elected officials. They need to step up to the task. They need to shun lobbyists and their disproportionate and generally harmful influence. They must do honest work each and every day to move the country and its people forward; to set aside their self-interest, personal and petty agendas in favor of the interests of the people. They're OUR elected officials and they need to represent US.

This country has "good bones," it's built to last through good times and bad. We're still a young, strong nation with lots of potential. And like a novice boxer with beginner's success and overconfidence; we don't want to be knocked out early in the fight.

As long as we continue electing pretenders, tricksters "smoke-and-mirrors" practitioners, and frauds we will continue on our downward slide. But if we elect seriously committed patriotic leaders with a vision of reviving the *America* of moral integrity, economic prowess, social and cultural leadership we have a chance.

We also need leaders who can subordinate their own egos, self-interest, and lust for power. Leaders who despite partisan differences can work together for the benefit of the nation. As a positive offshoot of the crippling and potentially disastrous battle of the budget and debt ceiling in 2013 new candidates began to emphasize their congeniality, compatibility and ability to work with people of all views to achieve overriding objectives.

We know the outrage and public disgust with stubborn politicians who refuse to talk or compromise. Partisan delays and roadblocks may not be so patiently tolerated in the future. It's a fast moving world and it requires political leaders and politicians who can efficiently and effectively come to agreement to advance the country's agenda and objectives.

This government is OF the People, BY the People and FOR the people. It's not DONE TO or AGAINST the people. Take your responsibility in governance seriously, or it will be hijacked from you. Despots and dictators thrive in an environment of discouragement, passivity, and non-involvement. Don't wait for oppression and a Revolution. Demand responsible Reformation and Reinvigoration.

As Americans do we really want to be dumber, poorer, sicker, and less competitive than our first world counterparts? Are we aiming for the title of "Least Improved?" From all indications we seem to be going backwards while other nations are advancing. Admittedly, improvement is tougher to attain from a higher level, and other nations would love to knock us off our pedestal, but why should we help them? Do we prefer excuses to performance? Or can we learn from our failures as we apparently have collectively failed to benefit from our successes?

It takes guts to be an American. And, to a great extent, far more than you may appreciate, you're responsible for the future of our country. Defend your Rights and the Rights of others. Don't let greedy or misguided politicians or government officials fleece you and promote anxiety and fear in your life.

Don't tolerate corruption or laziness in government. Resist the impulse to scapegoat and condemn groups of people without knowing the facts. Most of all PARTICIPATE. They don't call it a Participative Democracy for nothing.

Throughout this book I've tried my best to be as factual and apolitical as possible. It's easy for me because I don't fully support or trust either major party and I'm not affiliated with any of the splinter groups. But my concern and disgust with the current condition of our government is obvious, as are my personal views about the urgent necessity for action and reform.

As Americans we've always been able to overcome adversity, redefine and re-invent ourselves. Here we are in the most challenging days of our young country's history. Bold actions and expert leadership are required but we don't have them. Time is not on our side. The trends are clear. It's up to the people to close ranks and demand reform. Otherwise we will have enjoyed a brief but spectacular period of prosperity and world preeminence and confront a precipitous, disastrous downfall.

We're all counting on YOU!

Our relationship with our government is generally a long one. Think of it this way: The government was there when you were born and it will be there when you die. It was there when your parents, and their parents, were born too. When they got married, bought a house, had a career, invested their savings, became ill and passed away. It is involved in every major life event of you and your family. It often seems it's only there to sanctify or collect tribute, but it's also there to protect and provide structure. It may be our most enduring relationship with the exception of any spiritual or religious beliefs. Like a marriage we expect its love and support in exchange for ours. So, as in any relationship we feel betrayed when it cheats on us, doesn't care about our well-being or fails hold up its end of the bargain. Once the relationship has been abused or severed it will be difficult to repair and make whole. And both parties need to appreciate this simple fact.

--the author

Appendices, Exhibits,

Sources and Resources,

Index

If the freedom of speech is taken away then dumb and silent we may be led, like sheep to the slaughter.

--George Washington

The Constitution is the guide which I never will abandon.

--George Washington

A little group of willful men, representing no opinion but their own, have rendered the great government of the United States helpless and contemptible.

--Woodrow Wilson

Wealth can only be accumulated by the earnings of industry and the savings of frugality.

--John Tyler

Appendix A

Synopsis of the Constitution

The Constitution begins with the above three words. It is the start of the Preamble which explains "WHY" the document was written. It emphasizes the primary reasons: To create a "more perfect" government; that the government will be fair and just; that it was established to benefit the people and to protect us from internal strife and external attack; and that it would do so for future generations.

The document is divided into Articles and Sections.

Article I establishes the first of three branches of government, the Legislative. It also defines the roles and responsibilities of the House (of Representatives) and Senate, along with requirements for and limitations on officials of these bodies, and basic procedural requirements. It explains how the actions of these bodies can be codified into law.

Article II establishes the Executive Branch of government. It includes a method of election, term limits, minimum requirements for office holders, and describes the powers and responsibilities of this branch. Importantly, this article (sec. 2) outlines essential powers of the President including the role of Commander-in-Chief of the armed forces, the authority to pardon criminals, authority to name judges and other members of government (with approval of the Senate).

[223]

It also requires the President to make a State of the Union address, to interact with Congress and to act as Head of State in foreign diplomatic relations, and to ensure the laws of the United States are carried out (sec. 3). Section 4 provides for the removal of a President through the impeachment process.

Article III establishes the Judiciary branch. It provides for a Supreme Court to be the highest court in the land. It sets terms of judges, the kinds of cases that may be heard, and guarantees trials by jury in criminal cases.

Article IV concerns the states. This article guarantees that there will be equal and fair justice within and across state lines, provides for admittance of new states into the union, and the control of federal lands. It further defines our type of government as a republican form (often interpreted as a "representative democracy"). It emphasizes that the state derives its power from the people (sec. 4) and that the federal government will protect states from invasion or insurrection.

Article V provides for amendments to the constitution (the first ten are the Bill of Rights).

Article VI guarantees the payments of debts and contractual obligations of the United States. It designates the Constitution, laws and treaties to.be the supreme law of the nation. It requires officers of the federal and state governments to swear an "oath of allegiance" to the country and its Constitution when taking office

Article VII provides the mechanism for ratification, acceptance and enactment of the Constitution.

NOTE: The above is my _very_ abbreviated synopsis. I recommend that you read the original document in its entirety. Booklets containing the full constitution and all amendments are readily available either online or from the *U.S. Government Bookstore* at nominal cost.

Appendix B

How Laws are Made
(How a Bill Becomes Law)

1. Legislation is introduced into the House of Representatives or U.S. Senate – (procedures vary).
2. The bill is assigned to the appropriate Committee (Committee actions may include research, discussion, amendment(s), sub-committee assignments, hearings, etc.).
3. The bill is calendared for Floor action including discussion and debate, and vote.
4. If approved, the bill goes to the other chamber (House or Senate) for vote.
5. If not approved a Conference Committee will attempt to work out differences.
6. The Conference Report must be approved by both legislative bodies.
7. If approved, the bill goes to the President.
8. The President either signs, vetoes and sends it back to Congress or does nothing (pocket veto).
9. If signed by the President it becomes law, or if Congress overrides a Presidential veto.

Note: This is a very condensed version of a quite complex process. Interested readers are encouraged by the author to seek further information from the *Library of Congress* website at www.congress.gov.

Government, even in its best state, is but a necessary evil; in its worst state, an intolerable one.

--Thomas Paine

Any change is resisted because bureaucrats have a vested interest in the chaos in which they exist.

--Richard M. Nixon

The dangers of a concentration of all power in the general government of a confederacy so vast as ours are too obvious to be disregarded.

--Franklin Pierce

It is only when the people become ignorant and corrupt, when they degenerate into a populace, that they are incapable of exercising their sovereignty.

--James Monroe

Appendix C

A Concept for Participative Planning to Address National Priorities

I've toyed with this idea for a while now. If our federal government is essentially immobilized as a result of partisan politics, money from lobbyists, PACs, special interests, and personal ineptness, maybe we should enter into the process more aggressively. My thoughts are something like this:

1) Create National Priority Committees at the state level.

2) Use a jury selection model to identify citizens to participate.

3) Compensate volunteers for loss of wages and incidentals.

4) Assign these NPC's to work on major problems that require a substantial push.

5) Provide them with deadlines, education (in the problem area) resources and expert input. Insulate them from outside influence; prohibit them from taking money.

6) Arrange for the State NP Committees to provide their recommendations to Congress.

7) Widely publicize the process, recommendations and results.

I'm confident that we would see more objective, faster and better results. Let them attack the Economy first. We trust the Jury system to arrive at sound, expeditious decisions, and the process is a marvel.

Congressional officeholders are not generally that much better prepared to address national problems, and they're certainly more biased.

Like a jury the NPC members would listen to the evidence and expert testimony. They would weigh the options and make their recommendations. Congress would know the will of the people and certainly have less biased and filtered information than they've ever had. They would vigorously resist this model, however. They would view it as erosion of their Constitutional role. Privately they would bemoan the loss of a subjective, bi-ased, money-greased system that has worked so well for them, although not always for the country.

Think about it. It gives new meaning to the term "participative democracy."

Sources and Resources

"A Closeup Look at Congressional Wealth," WP Politics, *Washington Post*, www.washingtonpost.com, (undated/interactive).

Adams, Caralee J., "Most Students Aren't Ready for College, ACT Data Show, *Education Week*, (August 22, 2013), www.edwek.org.

AlterNet, "10 of the Biggest Tax Cheats in America," *www.alternet.org*, retrieved August 26, 2013.

American Customer Satisfaction Survey Index, *www.theacsi.org* , (2012 report)

American Foreign Service Association, www.afsa.org

"ATF's Fast and Furious scandal," (a compilation of articles). www.latimes.com

"Average Wages and Salaries of Employees in State and Local Government, Military and Private Sectors," *Tax Foundation*, www.taxfoundation.org (2007).

Avik, Roy, "Yet Another White House Obamacare Delay: Out of Pocket Caps Waived Until 2015," (contributor), *Forbes*, www.forbes.com, August 13, 2013.

Badnarik, Michael: Presentation on Bill of Rights to County Sheriffs, (vid.)youtube.com/watch?v=CENg_bS77f0&feature=youtube_gdata_player, Jan. 20, 2012.

Bastiat, Frederic, *The Law*, (La Loi), BN Publishing, Le Vergne, Tenn., (2007). Orig pub: 1849.

Bartlett, Bruce, "What People Think About Taxes," *New York Times*, April 16, 2013.

Belasco, James A., *Teaching the Elephant to Dance*, Crown Pub., New York, 1990.

Benn, E, Borns P, and McGory, K, "U.S.: Obamacare cost below forecast," Miami Herald, p.1a, September, 25, 2013.

Bible, King James version, 22:20-22

Bidwell, Allie, "Majority of Americans say Corruption has Increased," *US News and World Report*, July 10, 2013.

"Biggest Sex Scandals in Politics," Chicago Tribune, National Politics Section, www.chicagotribune.com, (undated)

Borns, Patricia & Chang, Daniel, "Obamacare Enrollees become urban legend," Miami Herald, October 14, 2013. p.1a.

Bradfprd, Hazel, "Budget puts military pension plan in crosshairs," www.pionline.com/article/20120123/PRINTSUB/301239975, January 23, 2012.

Brainy Quotes, *www.brainyquotes.com*.

Brown, Emma and Bui, Lynn, "Not Many Test Takers Ready for College," Washington Post Service, *Miami Herald*, August 22, 2013, p.4a.

Brudnik, Ida, "Congressional Salaries and Allowances," *Congressional Research Service*, www.library.clerk.house.gov., Jan. 15, 2013.

Buffet, Warren E, "A Minimum Tax For The Wealthy," *The New York Times*, (op-ed.), November 25, 2012.

Cassidy, John, "Demonizing Edward Snowden: Which Side are You On?" *New Yorker*, June 24, 2013

Cauchon, Dennis, "Some federal pensions pay handsome rewards," USA Today, http://usatoday30.usatoday.com/money/perfi/retirement/story/2012-07-19/federal-pensions-in-excess-of-100-thousand/57059716/1, September 15, 2012.

Center on Budget and Policy Priorities, *www.cbpp.org*.

Center for Range Voting, "U.S. Presidents and Election Fraud," *www.rangevoting.org*.

Chu, Ben, "Get your fiscal house in order: China warns U.S. as superpower expresses concern for $1.3tn of investments," the *Independent*, www.independent.co.uk/news/world/americas/get-your-fiscal-house-in-order-china-warns-us-as-superpower-expresses-concern-for-13tn-of-investments-8864935.html, October 7, 2013.

CNN, "Thought it was a Clean Bill? Not so fast –lots of pork in there," Washington, October 17, 2013.

"Computer Upgrade Nlamed for Nationwide EBT System Shutdown on Saturday," *CBS,* October 12, 2013).

Condon, Stephanie, "Ron Paul Proposes Saving $1T by Scrapping Five Federal Department," CBS NEWS, *www.cbsnews.com/8301-503544_162-20121485-503544.html*, October 17, 2011.

Congress, *www.congress.gov*.

Congressional Assets-Special Report, WP Politics, Washington Post, www.washingtonpost.com, October 6, 2012. http://colorlines.com/archives/2013/01/113th_congress_diversity.html

Congressional Budget Office, *www.CBO.org*

Contact Elected Officials, *www.usa.gov/contact/elected.*

Contact Your Government, *www.usa.gov*

"Constitution" (of the United States), *www.archieves.gov/exhibits/charters/constitution.*

Cook, Walter Wheeler, "Act, Intention, and Motive in Criminal Law," *The Yale Law Journal*, p.645-663.

"Corruption Perceptions Index," prepared by *Transparency International,*www.cpi.transparency.org,

Cost of Living (The)," *DePaul University*, www..depaul.edu/djabon/cpi.htm

"Cost of War to the United States (The)," *costofwar.com.*

Coulson, Andrew, "A Picture is Wort $300 Billion," *Cato Institute*, www.cato.org/blog/picture-worth-300-billion, September 9, 2009.

"Customer Service Standards for U.S. Government and Federal Employees," from Archive, *www.govinfo.library.unt.edu/npr/custserv/1997.*

Dann, Carrie, "How America Tallies its 11.1 Million Undocumented Immigrants," *nbcpolitics.nbcnews.com,* April 11, 2013.

Demographic Data and Reports, www.census.gov.

Depatment of Justice, www.doj.gov.

Diamond, Gregg, (songwriter) & True, Andrea (singer), *More More More*, from *Last Days of Disco*, (1976) ww.stlyrics.com/lyrics/lastdaysofdisco/moremoremorept1.html (Recording).

Dorning, Mike and Strohm, Chris, "Obama Credibility At Risk," Miami Herald, August 25, 2013, p19A.

Dubner, Stephen J, "How Biased is Your Media?": A Freakonomics Podcast, Stephen J. Dubner, *www.freakonomics.com*, February 16, 2012

Editor, *The Washington Times*, "The pension bubble," www.washingtontimes.com/news/2012/jun/29/the-pension-bubble/, June 29, 2012.

Editorial Board, *"Social Security Present and Future,"*New York Times, Sunday Section, March 30,2013.

Education, Department of, www.DOE.gov.

Eisenhower, Susan, "50 Years Later We're Still Ignoring Ike's Warning," *New York Post*, January 16, 2011. *www.washingtonpost.com*, Retreived 8/26/13

E21, Staff Editorial, *Economic Policies for the 21st Century*, "The U.S. and Europe: Government of Equal Size?" www.economics21.org/commentary/us-and-europe-governments-equal-size, February 8, 2012.

FactCheck.org,"Are Federal Workers Overpaid?" December1, 2010.

FBI Law Enforcement Bulletin, www.fbi.gov/stats.

Federal Emergency Management Agency, www.fema.gov.

Ferrera, Peter, "Look Out Below: The Obamacare Chaos is Coming," Contributor: Op.Ed., *Forbes*, April 7, 2013.

Foley, Elise, "Obama Deportation Toll Could Pass 2 Million at Current Rates,"Huffington Post, *www.huffingtonpost.com*, January 31, 2013.

Fontevecchia, Agustino, "Shutdown and Debt Ceiling Debate Prove U.S. Not Worthy of AAA Credit Rating: S&P," *Forbes*, http://www.forbes.com/sites/afontevecchia/2013/09/30/shutdown-and-debt-ceiling-debate-prove-u-s-doesnt-deserve-aaa-credit-rating-sp/, Sept. 30, 2013 (retrieved 10/1/13).

Fowler, E, "Presidential Ads 70 Percent Negative in 2012, Up from 9 Percent in 2008," Wesleyan Media Project, Wesleyan University, www.mediaproject.edu, May 2, 2012.

Fowler, Erika Fanklin and Ridout, Travis N, "Negative, Angry, and Ubiquitous: Political Advertising in 2012," Journal of Applied Research on Contemporary Politics, vol.10, (The Forum), Issue 4, 2013.

OUT TO GET YOU

Franz, Michael, "Issue Groups in Electoral Politics: 2012 In Context," Journal of Applied Research on Contemporary Politics, vol.10, (The Forum), Issue 4, 2013.

Gallup, "America's Most Admired Professions," *www.gallup.com/poll/1654/honesty-ethics-professions.aspx#4*, November 29, 2012. (retrieved 9/13/13).

Gallup, "Majority in U.S. Still Say Government Doing Too Much," *www.gallup.com/poll/157481/majority-say-government-doing.aspx*, September 17, 2012. (retrieved 9/22/13).

Gellman, Barton, "NSA Broke Privacy Rules Thousands of Times Per Year, Audit Finds," *Washington Post*, (National Security Section), August 15, 2013.

Ghazzali, Adus-Sattar, "A Decade of Civil Rights Erosion in America," *National Coaltion to Protect Civil Freedoms, Organization*, www.civilfreedoms.org, 8/25/2011.

Gladwell, Malcom," The Tipping Point: How Little Things Can Make a Big Difference," Back Bay Books, N.Y. (2002).

Greenberg, Duncan, Thibault, Marie, "America's Richest Families," *Forbes*, www.forbes.com, December 3, 2009.

Grynbaum, Michael M., "City Argues to Overturn Ruling That Prevented Limits on Sugary Drinks," *New York Times*, June 11, 2013

Halper, Daniel, The Weekly Standard,"U.S. Per Person Debt Now 35% Higher than that of Greece," *The Weekly Standard*, www.weeklystandard.com, Nov.5, 2012.

Hansen, Jesper Rosenberg and Viladsen, Anders R,"Comparing Public and Private Managers' Leadership Styles: Umderstanding The Role of Job Context," *Inrernational Public Management Journal*, Vol. 13, Issue 3, 2010, p. 247-274.

Hansen, Mary, "Top Five Criminal Motives," *www.loupdargent.info*.

Hartung, Adam, "Why the postal service is going out of business," *Forbes*, December 6, 2011.

Healthcare.gov, *www.healthcare.gov*.

(The) Heritage Foundation, *www.heritage.org*.

"Homeland Security Spending Since 2001," *National Priorities Project, A Peoples Guide to the Federal Budget*, www.nationalpriorities.org., Feb. 28, 2013.

"House GOP chairman accuses IRS of obstructing investigation into tea party targeting." A.P.(Associated Press), as reported in the *Washington Post,* August 2, 2013.

Huang & Frentz, "Myths and Realities about the Estate Tax," *Center on Budget and Policy Priorities*, www.cbpp.org/files/estatetaxmyths.pdf, August 29, 2013.

Huff, Darrell, *How to Lie with Statistics*, pub: W.W. Norton & Co.,1993 (reissue)

Ignatius, David, "Americans Don't Like 'Big Brother," David Ignatius, *Miami Herald*, July 29, 2013, p.13A

Info Please, "U.S. Postal Service Motto," www.infoplease.com/askeds/post-office-motto.html

Irwin,Neil, "Why Japan is the Most Interesting Story in Global Economics Right Now," *Washington Post*, April 8, 2013.

Isaacs, Katelin, "Retirement Benefits for Members of Congress,"*Congressional Research Service*, www.senate.gov/CRSReports/crs-publish.cfm?pid='0E%2C*PLC8"%40 %0A, August 9, 2013

Iserbyt, Charlotte T, *The Deliberate Dumbing Down of America*, Conscience Press, 1999.

Jackson, David, "Obama once oppose raising debt ceiling," *USA Today*, www.onlinecontent.usatoday.com/communities/theoval/post/2011/01/obama-once-opposed-lifting-debt-ceiling/1#.UlV93hAQO_c, January 6, 2011.

Jaschik, Scott, "On Pace With Inflation," *Inside Higher Ed*, www.insidehighered.com/news/2013/04/08/aaup-survey-finds-average-faculty-salary-increased-rate-inflation-last-year

Justice News, *Department of Justice*, "Medicare Fraud Strike Force Charges 89 Individuals for Approximately $223 Million in False Billing," www.justice.gov, May 14, 2013.

Kane, Jason, "Health Costs: How the U.S. Compares with Other Countries," *PBS NewsHour*, www.pbs.org/newshour/rundown/2012/health-costs, October 22, 2012.

Keller, Sara, Schanz, Deborah, Beisheim, Otto, "Measuring Tax Attractiveness Across Countries," (working paper/academic), *Besheim School of Management, and Ludwig Maximilians University*, econstor.eu, June 9, 2013.

Koff, Rochelle, "Is Marijuana less harmful than Alcohol? *Miami Herald*, August 26, 2013, p.1a

Kohn, Sally, "The 113th Congress and the Tryanny of the Minority," *Colorlines*, January 18, 2013, *www.coorlines.com*.

Kumar, Nikhil, "U.S. Budget Battle: IMF's Christine Lagarde warns America's lawmakers they risk pushing world int recession," *The Independent*, http://www.independent.co.uk/news/world/americas/us-budget-battle-imfs, October 14, 2013.

Larvie, Ken, "The Manipulation of the American Mind: Like butter with a hot knife," *www.examiner.com*, November 21, 2012

Law Enforcement Journal, jghcs.info.

Leonhardt, David, "The German Example," *The New York Times*, June 7, 2011.

Library of Congress, *www.loc.gov*.

Lincoln, Abraham, "Gettysburg Address," November 19, 1863, Gettysburg, Pennsylvania, *www.abrahamlincolnonline.org*

Linn Allison, "A teen job becomes a rarity in U.S. economy," Today (Money*) CNBC, www.today.com,* May 3, 2012.

Liptak, Adam, "Justices 5-4 Reject Corporate Spending Limit," *New York Times*, www.nytimes.com/2010/01/22/us/politics/22scotus.html?pagewanted=all&_r=0, January 21, 2010.

Loder, Asjylyn Fracking Boosts Oil Production to Highest Level in Twenty Years," *Bloomberg*, www.bloomberg.com, July 10, 2013.

MacAskill, Ewen, "NSA Paid Millions to Cover Prism Compliance Costs for Tech Companies, *The Guardian*, August 22, 2013.

Manning, Jennifer E, CRS Report for Congress, "Membership of the 113th Congress, A Profile," *Congressional Research Service*, August 5, 2013.

McCarthy, Anna, "When I;m 65:A Retirement Timeline," *Mother Jones*, www.motherjones.com/politics/2009/05/when-im-65-retirement-timeline, May/June, 2009.

McCoy, Peter, "Bill Clinton's drive to increase home ownership went way too far," *Businessweek*, February 27, 2008.

McCartney Robert, "Federal shutdown idles Air Force expert honored for saving Government $1 billion," Washington Post, *www.washingtonpost.com/local/federal-shutdown-idles-air-force-expert-honored-for-saving-government-1-*

billion/2013/10/02/a73a6ece-2b94-11e3-97a3-
ff2758228523_story.html?wpmk=MK0000200, October 2, 2013.

McLoed, Stephen, "In Criminal Law Motive Does Matter, McLoed, Stephen, *New York Times* (Letter to the Editor), April 8, 1999.

Mendes, Elizabeth, "American's Satisfaction with U.S. Remains Near 32-Year Low," *Gallup Politics*, September 28, 2011.

Meriam-Webster Dictionary (Trick/Trickster definitions), retrieved 8/15/2013. *Meri-amwebster.com.*

Merrifield, Clark and Streib, Lauren, "America's Most Corrupt Industries," *The Daily Beast*, www.thedailybeast.com, April 27, 2010.

Montgomery, Lori, and Kane, Paul, "Stalemate Forces First Government Closure in 17 Years," Washington Post, *www.washingtonpost.com/politics*, October 1, 2013.

Moore, David S. *Statistics: Concepts and Controversies.* Fourth Ed. New York: W. H. Freeman and Company, 1997.

Moore, Stephen, "The Budget Sequester is a Success," *Wall Street Journal*, (Opinion), August 13, 2013.

Moore, Steve, "The Number of People Working in Government, Manufacturing is Almost a Complete Reversal of Pattern in 1960,"*Tampa Bay Times*, Politifact.com, April 1, 2011.

"Most Important Problem," *Gallup*, survey: www.gallup.com/poll/1675, July 10-14, 2013.

Mui, Ylan Q, "Markets Jump to Record High on Fed Decision to Keep Stimulus," *The Washington Post*, www.washintonpost.com, Sept. 18, 2013. (retrieved 9/18/13).

Naturalization Self Test, US Citizenship and Immigration Services, www.uscis.gov/portal/site/uscis.

Neyfakh, Leon, "Robert Reich takes his fight to the Big Screen," *Boston Globe*, (Arts/Movies,1), September 21, 2013.

"Norway Has Best Living Standards; Niger Worst," Marketing Charts from data by *United Nations Development Programme, www.marketingcharts.com,* October 6, 2009.

Obama, Barack, President's News Conference, (at the White House), August 9, 2013.

Obama-Care, *www.obama-care.org.*

OECD, "Growing Unequal? Income Distribution and Poverty in OECD Countries," Organization for Economic Cooperation and Development, 2008. p. 112.

OpenSecrets.org, Center for Responsive Politics, *www.opensecrets.org.*

Ordonez, Franco, "Deportations Boost Call Centers," *Miami Herald*, p.1A, September 2, 2013.

Orfield, Gary, Prof., *UCLA Civil Rights Project*, (excerpt) May. 2003.

Organization for Economic Cooperation and Development, www.oecd.org.

Paranoia," (definition of) Urban Dictionary, *www.urbandictionary.com/define.php?term=paranoia.*

Park, Abraham, PhD, "Why did Subprime become such a Big Deal?" *Graziado Business Review*, Pepperdine University, www.gbr.pepperdine.edu.

"Personal Income Tax Rates," *Global Finance Magazine* http://www.gfmag.com/tools/global-database/economic-data/12151-personal-income-tax-rates.html#axzz2hKt4vmbC (2012).

Pilkington, Ed, "Declassified NSA files show agency spied on Muhammad Ali and MLK,The Guardian, *www.theguardian.com,* September 26, 2013. (retrieved 9/26/13).

Pinchot, Gifford and Elizabeth, *The End of Bureacracy and the Rise of the Intelligent Organization*, Berrett-Koehler Pub., 1993.

Plumer, Brad, "Who receives government benefits, in six charts," *Washington Post*, September 18, 2012.

Pollock, Richard, "Canadian firm hired to build troubled Obamacare exchanges," *Washington Times*, http://washingtonexaminer.com/canadian-firm, October 4, 2013.

Porter, Eduardo, "Economic Health? It's Relative," *The New York Times*, October 16, 2012.

Putin, Vladimir V, "A Plea For Caution From Russia," *The New York Times*, (Opinion Pages), September 11, 2013.

Readers Digest (Canada), "Canada's Most Trusted Professions: 2012" *www.readersdigest.ca/magazine/2013-trust-poll/canadas-most-trusted-professions-2012-trust-poll-results* . (accessed 9/15/13).

Reich, Robert, "America's Biggest Jobs Program: The U.S. Military," *Christian Science Monitor*, August 13, 2010.

Roff, Peter, "Pelosi: Pass Healthcare Reform So You Can Find Out What's In It," *U.S. News and World Report*, March 9, 2010.

Rosen-Amy, Sam, "Congress Passes Year's First Spending Bill With Plenty of Riders, Declares Pizza a Vegetable," *Center for Effective Government*, www.centerfor effec-tivegovt.org, November 21, 2011.

Rosenberg, Carol, "Guantanamo's Tab: $2.7M per prisoner," *Miami Herald,* July 31, 2013, pg. A1

Rosenthal, Elisabeth, "Just How Affordable Will Obamacare be?." *Seattle Times*, http://mobile.seattletimes.com/story/today/2021921954/track-ip_news_lite-1.2.2-./, October 4, 2013.

Rothwell, Steve, and Sweet, Ken, "In Past Shutdowns Stocks Survived," *Miami Herald*, September 29, 2013, (p.C1).

Sanchanta, Mariio & Chow, Jason, "U.S. Expats Balk at Tax Law: American Citizenship Renuciations are Soaring," *Wall Street Journal*, August 12, 2013.

Sauter, Michael B, and Stockdale, Charles B, "America's Least Corrupt States," *24/7 Wall St*, www.wallst.com, posted March 22, 2012.

Sauter, Michael B., and Stockdale, Charles B, "America's Most Corrupt States," *Center for Public Integrity*, FoxBusiness Report, www.foxbusiness.com, pub. 24/7WallStreet, March 22, 2012.

Shear, Michael, "Obama and Clintons Share Stage for Healthcare Talk, *New York Times, September 24, 2013.*

Schulz, Thomas, "How the German Economy Became a Model," *Spiegel Online*, *www.spiegel.de/international/business/the-us-discovers-germany...a-822167.html*, March 21, 2012.

Schuman, Daniel, "Congress Deserves a Big Fat Raise: We Loathe Them, Their Work Stinks, It's Time We Paid Them Better," *MSNBC*, www.slate.com, April 2, 2013.

"Sequester (The): What you need to know," *http://www.whitehouse.gov/issues/sequester*.

Shackford, Scott, 3 Reasons the 'Nothing to Hide' Crowd Should be Worried About Government Surveillance," *reason.com*, June 12, 2013.

OUT TO GET YOU

"Shark Tank," ABC TV show, *www.abc.go.com/shows*.

Siegel, Michael, *The President as Leader*, Pearson Pub, 2011.

60 Minutes, (with Steve Kroft), "*Disability USA*," aired on *CBS* October 6, 2013.

Solomon,John and Wolfgang, Ben, "The Long Line of Conservatives Targeted by the IRS," Washington Times, *www.washingtontimes.com/news/2013/oct/3/irs-targeted-dr-ben-carson-after-prayer-breakfast-/*, Octber 3, 2013.

Sorock, Ann, "The Congressional Wealth Gap," *Legal Insuurection*, www.legalinsurrection.com, August 2, 2012.

Stone, Andrea, "Social Media Reference Guide for DHS Analysts," Department of Homeland Security, National Operations Center,Media Monitoring Capability, Desktop Reference Binder, *http://www.scribd.com/doc/82701103/Analyst-Desktop-Binder-REDACTED*, 2011, p. 21-22. (retrieved 9/25/13).

Survey of Presidential Leadership, C-Span, *www.americanpresidents.org/survey/historians/overall.asp*, 2013. (reteived 8/31/2013).
Swann, Christopher and Pethokoukis, "An Inevitable Slide in America's Standard of Living," *New York Times* (Business Day), October 7, 2010.

Swarns, Rachael L, "Failed Amnesty Legislation of 1986 Haunts the Current Immigration Bills in Congress," *New York Times*, May 23, 2006.

Thurston, Susan, Obamacare to cost big companies money, time," Tampa Bay Times, www.tampabay.com/news/business/banking/obamacare-to-cost-big-companies-money-time/2145535, October 4, 2013.

Toscano, Paul and Weinberger, Jill, "The 10 Biggest Government Contractors," *CNBC*, www.cnbc.com, June 13, 2012.

Trotta, Daniel, "Iraq War Costs U.S. More Than 2 Trillion: Study," *www.reuters.com/article/2013/03/14/us-iraq-war-anniversary*, March14, 2013.

Turchin, Peter and Nefedov, Sergey, *Secular Cycles,* Princeton University Press, N.J. (2009).

24/7WallSt., "TheMost Educated Countries in the World," *www.247wallst.com*, Sept. 21, 2012, (accessed 9/3/13).

Urban Dictionary, *www.urbandictionary.com* (for definition of the term: Paranoia) accessed on 8/8/13.

U.S.Army, Benefits,

OUT TO GET YOU

www.goarmy.com/benefits/total-compensation.html.

U.S. Government Bookstore, *gpo.gov*

U.S. Office of Management and Budget, *www.whitehouse.gov/omb.*

U.S. Department of Agriculture, www.USDA.gov.

U.S. Department of Defense, www.defense.gov.

U.S. Department of Education, *www.ed.org*

U.S. Department of Health and Human Services, *www.hhs.gov.*

Vanderbilt Business, (Vanderbilt University)
http://www.vanderbilt.edu/magazines/vanderbilt-business

www.Votesmart.org

Wall Street Journal, (Review and Outlook), "Congress's ObamaCare Exemption," *http://online.wsj.com/article/SB10001424127887324635904578644202946287548.ht ml#articleTabs%3Dcomments,* August 5, 2013, (accessed on 9/24/13).

Wallison, Peter J., and Pinto, Edward J., "A Government Mandated Housing Bubble," *Forbes*, February 16, 2009

Wang, Sam, "Gerrymanders, Part 1:Busting both-sides-do-it-myth," http://election.princeton.edu/2012/12/30/gerrymanders-part-1-busting-the-both-sides-do-it-myth/.

Weaver, Jay, "Miami Doctor and Therapists Charged With $63 Million MediCare Fraud," Miami Herald, July 17, 2013.

Weintraub, Lynne, "Newsweek asks: How Dumb are We?" *www.newsweek.com/2011/03/20/how-dumb-are-we/html.,* March 20,2011

Weissman, Jordan, "The Real Problem with Welfare: It Stopped Helping the Poor," Atlantic Monthly, August 8, 2012.

Wells, Carrie, "Ben Carson says he was targeted by IRS for his beliefs," Baltimore Sun, *ws/bs-md-ben-carson-irs-20131003_1_irs-audit-irs-controversy-ben-carson,* October 3, 2013.

White House, *www.whitehouse.gov.*

"Who Represents You in the U.S. Congress?" *www.whoismyrepresentative.com.*

OUT TO GET YOU

Wood, Robert W., "U.S. Tax System Ranks 94th Out of 100—Right Below Zimbabwae," *Forbes*, July 12, 2013.

World Crime Statistics (U.N. Report – 2010), *www.unodc.org.fv.*

World Fact Book, www.cia.gov.

Worstall, Tim, Why the Fair Tax will Fail," *Forbes*, August 22, 2012.

Yen, Hope, "4 in 5 in U.S. Face Near Poverty, No work," *Associated Press*, AP.org, July 28, 2013.

Yoder, Eric, "Despite salary rate freeze, average federal salary rises," *The Washington Post*, www.wahington post.com, April 9, 2013. (retrieved 9/17/13)

York, Byron, "Where's the sense of crisin in a 17% Government Shutdown," *Washington Examiner*, http://washingtonexaminer.com/wheres-sense-of-crisis-in-a-17-percent-government-shutdown/article/2536862, October 5, 2013.

Yost, Peter, "Holder Proposes Changes in Criminal Justice System," *Associated Press*, Yahoo News, August 12, 2013.

I am not worried about the deficit. It is big enough to take care of itself.

-- Ronald Reagan

These stories about my intellectual capacity really get under my skin.
You know, for a while
I even thought my staff believed it.
There on my schedule first thing every morning it said,
"Intelligence Briefing."

--George W. Bush

I just received the following wire from my generous Daddy:
"Dear Jack, Don't buy a single vote more than is necessary.
I'll be damned if I'm going to pay for a landslide."

-- John Kennedy

Being president is like being a jackass in a hailstorm.
There's nothing to do but to stand there and take it.

--Lyndon Johnson

INDEX

Now it's my turn...

Would you like an easy, glamorous job
with lots of benefits and many opportunities
to enrich yourself and your friends?
--consider Politics.

If you live in this Country for more than a week,
you'll discover that the illusion is at
complete odds with the reality.

A slogan during the Vietnam War was:
"America, love it or leave it!"
An appropriate slogan for today might be:
"America, love it and fix it!"

It isn't only Hollywood
that provides entertainment to the world.
Washington D.C. does a good job too!

U.S. Government: A colossal Game Show
where the players make up the rules,
and the audience always loses.

--the author

About the Author

Dr. BEN A. CARLSEN, MBA is author of several books and hundreds of articles. He is a writer, educator, businessman, manager, and consultant. "Dr. Ben," as he's known to his students, earned his Bachelor's Degree at the *University of Washington*, an MBA at *Pepperdine University*, and a Doctorate at the *University of San Francisco*. He has management experience in both the public and private sectors. Dr. Carlsen served as Chairman of the *Productivity Managers Network* in *Los Angeles County*, as well as on numerous professional and non-profit organizations and advisory boards.

Dr. Carlsen taught at *California State University*, the *University of California*, *University of San Francisco*, *Western International University*, *University of Phoenix* (*Axia College*), and *Corinthian Colleges*. He has a personal and professional interest in business, political and social issues, organizational leadership, management, economics and finance.

Dr. Ben now lives in *Miami* and enjoys writing books and articles, reading and research, exercise at the beach each morning, spending time with friends, and is a movie buff.

He is proud to be an independent thinker and voter.

*Life, faculties, production—in other words,
individuality, liberty, property -- this is man.
And in spite of the cunning of artful political leaders,
these three gifts from God precede all human
legislation and are superior to it.*

-----

*Everyone wants to live at the expense of the state. They
forget that the state lives at the expense of everyone.*

--Frederic Bastiat

If you liked this book here are some other titles by the same author:

Is it all a game? Are your personal finances part of a larger economic contest? Can you learn to play the game more effectively and win? *Money Game Winner* takes a unique new look at our attitudes towards money and taps into our competitive nature to achieve financial success.

Are you an overspender? Do you know someone who is? If you answered no to both questions you must be a frugal hermit. Learn the symptoms, diagnosis and strategies for treating this pervasive disorder. Gain control of your spending and your life!

Out to get you!

Before you can improve your finances you must survive. *Personal Financial Survival* is intended for readers having financial difficulties and seeking to turn their finances around. Lots of tips and advice. Readers love this book!

Bites of Business is exactly that! A collection of "bite-size" articles designed to improve your business and managerial skills. It's all covered-- everything from customer relations, human resources, sales and profit, accounting, performance improvement and ethics. A great book for new, aspiring or seasoned managers.

Available only in eBook format this short book lists the major (avoidable) financial mistakes that people make. These mistakes can ruin your finances – Learn what they are, and how not to make them!

If you have ever considered an internet home-based business, particularly an MLM (multi-level marketing) type you should read this eBook first.

Yes, it's a "Vampire Book" but one for thinking teens and adults. In it vampires make inroads into the healthcare business. After all, that's where the blood is!

Out to get you!

Government is not reason; it is not eloquent; it is force. Like fire, it is a dangerous servant and a fearful master.

-George Washington

The care of human life and happiness, and not their destruction, is the first and only object of good government.

--Thomas Jefferson

When they call the roll in the Senate, the Senators do not know whether to answer 'Present' or 'Not guilty.'

--Theodore Roosevelt

There is more selfishness and less principle among members of Congress than I had any conception of, before I became President of the U.S.

--James K. Polk

Out to get you!

All of Dr. Ben Carlsen's books are available at
Amazon.com.

Hardcover or paperback editions are also
available at *BN.com* (*Barnes & Noble*) **and,**
through *Ingram Book Distributors*,
at bookstores everywhere.

Out to get you!

No man is good enough to govern another man
without the other's consent.

-Abraham Lincoln

Power concedes nothing without a demand.
It never did, and it never will.
Find out just what people will submit to, and you have
found out the exact amount of injustice and wrong
which will be imposed upon them; and these will con-
tinue till they have resisted with either words or
blows, or with both.
The limits of tyrants are prescribed by the endurance
of those whom they suppress.

--Frederick Douglass

www.ingramcontent.com/pod-product-compliance
Lightning Source LLC
Chambersburg PA
CBHW030426290526
45786CB00001B/158